# Cases in Public Human Resource Management

## T. Zane Reeves
University of New Mexico

**F. E. Peacock Publishers, Inc.**
Itasca, Illinois

This book is dedicated to Robert Morgan Fox, whose courage and wit were a constant source of inspiration during its preparation.

*Advisory Editor in Public Administration*
Bernard H. Ross
School of Public Affairs
American University

# CONTENTS

## III. Human Resources Management

# PREFACE

This text is designed to meet the need among instructors who teach specialized courses in Public Sector Personnel Management, Human Resources Management, or Employment Relations for a supplemental book of case studies that could be used in these courses. It includes 30 cases from the following broad areas typically covered in the aforementioned courses, at either the graduate or undergraduate level:

- *Personnel Management:* Recruitment, Selection, Promotion, Job Evaluation, Compensation, Fair Labor Standards Act, Merit Systems Standards, Personnel Records Management, and Employee Benefits

- *Employment Relations:* Collective Bargaining, Labor-Management Relations, Affirmative Action, Sexual and Ethnic Harassment, Off-Duty Conduct, Privacy Issues, Due Process, and ADA Concerns

- *Human Resources Management:* Human Resources Planning, Performance Evaluation, Attendance Management, Employee Development and Training, Layoff and Reduction-in-Force, Discipline, Managing the Traditional Worker, Conflict Resolution and Grievance Handling, and Comparative Human Resources Management

One or more cases are presented in each of the aforementioned areas. They can be used as a teaching tool in the classroom, by trainers with employees, supervisors, or managers, as well as for provocation for individual analysis and self-assessment.

The attractiveness of each case for these purposes is enhanced by the following characteristics:

• *Authenticity:* Frequently, case studies seem "less realistic"—too academic, theoretical, or unrealistic to students because they are cast in obviously fictitious locales or imaginary governmental organizations, that is, Happy Valley, Circle City, Midwest City, and so forth. Cases used in this text are presented in the context of actual school districts, municipalities, counties, states, and federal agencies—in most cases, where the incidents occurred, for example, Los Angeles, Phoenix, Reno, Albuquerque, Tucson. Names of individuals have been changed, except in cases where real names would be obvious because of widespread publicity. Thus, care is taken to make the cases believable to the reader.

• *Content- and Process-Oriented Presentation:* Each case has the twofold objective of (1) teaching analytical and decision-making skills, and (2) more fully informing students and readers of the issues related to the problem addressed. In other words, each case can stand alone and does not presume that students will necessarily do additional background reading regarding the issue. Therefore, more information and explanatory detail is provided than is typically found in other case study readers. One of the frustrations expressed by students with shorter case studies is that they do not have sufficient information upon which to analyze the case or formulate a decision based on the options available. Students are exposed to subject-matter content as well as decision-making processes as the basis of discussion and group assessment exercises.

• *Distinctiveness of the Public Sector:* Although in some areas of human resources management there are close similarities among private- and public-sector organizations, in other subject-matter areas the differences are immense, for example, collective bargaining, job evaluation, merit systems standards, and discipline for cause. These differences are brought out when appropriate. Of course, the category "public sector" includes a rich plethora of diverse organizations, and the 30 case studies reflect all levels of special district, municipal, county, state, and federal agencies. This book also brings together cases from a variety of occupations and professions in areas such as law enforcement, social work, corrections, custodial, fire fighting, forestry, teaching, health care, and others, many of which are not widely found in the private sector.

Each case study is followed by discussion questions whereby the student, or a group of students, can be asked to respond from at least two different perspectives. On any single case study an instructor can assign students to analyze the problems, issues, and ethical dilemmas presented from different perspectives.

There is no Instructor's Manual for this book nor would one be feasibly prepared. There are no "right" answers presented, although there may be certain solutions that seem to the readers to be more risk free, logical, or fair. It is recommended that groups of students or trainees be assigned to work as consensus-building groups in order to develop a variety of perspectives on the issues raised.

I would be pleased to respond to your questions and receive your suggestions as well as nominations for future case studies to be included in the second edition. You can reach me at tzane@unm.edu.

# I

# PERSONNEL MANAGEMENT

# 1

## RECRUITMENT AND SELECTION

# Deer Valley Hires a New Coach

*Every basketball game is won by the team that scores the most points. How important is shooting? Let me put it this way—if you don't shoot well, you're going to spend a lot of time sitting at the end of the bench during games. I don't care who your old man is or how influential he may be; if you don't shoot well, you won't play basketball at Deer Valley High!*

It was bad enough for Dave Hollinger to learn that he had been fired as head boys basketball coach at Deer Valley High School (DVHS) in suburban Phoenix, despite a winning season. Hollinger also had suffered the humiliation of being informed that he would not be allowed to reapply for his old position, which was now vacant owing to an abrupt resignation by his successor. Coaches of boys and girls sports in the past had assumed that the Deer Valley Unified School District (DVUSD) would automatically renew their coaching contracts, unless there was just cause to remove them for poor performance. Removal of coaches had usually been preceded by notice of deficiencies and an opportunity to improve prior to termination.

Former Coach Hollinger believed that DVUSD breached its obligations under his employment agreement when it

3

removed him from his position without adequate notice or opportunity to correct any deficiencies. Further, Hollinger and the union grievance committee asserted that the district's failure to provide both predisciplinary notice and an opportunity to respond prior to removal resulted in violation of Hollinger's constitutional due process rights and that the district did not have just cause to terminate his contract as head basketball coach. More fundamentally, Hollinger was angry—he had taken a losing basketball program at Deer Valley and made it into a winner only to be fired as his thanks!

Finally, Hollinger was upset when DVUSD added insult to injury by engaging in an obvious reprisal when it failed to even consider him for a head coaching vacancy for the 1996–97 coaching season. Hollinger was prepared to sue the district, if necessary, in order to gain full reinstatement to his position as head basketball coach with all moneys (addenda and summer camp) lost due to the wrongful removal. In addition, Hollinger intended to ask that all adverse material related to his wrongful removal be expunged from the personnel file, supervisory file, and all evaluations maintained by DVUSD central personnel.

There was some glimmer of hope—Hollinger had requested and been granted one final hearing regarding his nonrenewal of contract. The district superintendent promised to explain his reasons for not allowing Hollinger to reapply for the coaching position that had once again become vacant.

## AN UNHAPPY TENURE IN DEER VALLEY

Dave Hollinger was hired as the head boys basketball coach at DVHS for the 1992–93, 1993–94, 1994–95, and 1995–96 school years. Hollinger's coaching record during these years was 15-5, 14-6, 13-12, and 12-11, respectively. Unfortunately for Hollinger, his teams had failed to defeat their district archrival, Barry Goldwater High School, during these four years. Despite winning seasons, there were indications that not everyone approved of Hollinger's coaching style. As a social studies teacher in the classroom, Hollinger was quite popular, but some parents and administrators thought Hollinger emphasized winning too much. Another parent, who also happened to be on the school board, believed that Hollinger did not appreciate the abilities of the board member's son as the "sixth man off the bench" for the basketball team. These groups conspired to have Hollinger removed as head basketball coach. There followed a series of events that ultimately would lead to Hollinger's demise:

1.    On March 12, 1993, Wayne Kimball, who was Hollinger's predecessor as head basketball coach and was currently athletic director, evaluated Hollinger's performance as coach during the 1992–93 season. Kimball subsequently recommended, without meeting with Hollinger, that his contract not be renewed for the 1993–94 season; Kimball's recommendation was not accepted by the superintendent, and Hollinger continued as head basketball coach for three additional years.

2.    In early October 1995, Hollinger and Deer Valley Education Association (DVEA) representative Betty Kim met with Dr. Joseph Schmit, principal of DVHS, to discuss mutual expectations. Hollinger wanted to avoid potential problems and was concerned that his coaching position might not be renewed the following year. Kim and Hollinger also met with DVUSD Superintendent Dr. Pat Sims and Associate Principal Jerry Simmons during October 1995. All parties agreed that these meetings were positive, with Simmons providing advice to Hollinger regarding ways to improve the basketball program.

3.    However, the relationship between Coach Hollinger and the district's administrators deteriorated rapidly during the 1995–96 basketball season. DVUSD administrators would later provide a number of instances during the basketball season in support of their contention that they had just cause to not renew Hollinger's contract as head basketball coach for the 1996–97 season.

In an attempt to force the issue, Hollinger applied for the vacant position. However, Hollinger was informed that his application could not be accepted for "personnel reasons." When pressed, the district provided the following incidents as the basis of its decision not to allow Hollinger to apply for the position of head boys basketball coach:

• Hollinger held an open gym for football players during football season.

- Hollinger encouraged track athletes to play club basketball instead of going out for track.

- Hollinger confronted Athletic Director Wayne Kimball regarding Junior Varsity Coach Cappelli's use of a defensive play during a JV game that Hollinger wished to use in the varsity game.

- Hollinger argued with players or had bad player relationships in past years.

- Hollinger allowed basketball players to drive their own vehicles to the Paradise Valley game rather than riding with their parents.

- Hollinger conducted an inappropriate "ass chewing" of players during halftime at an away game in Yuma.

- Hollinger's relationship with coaches in the region suffered because he did not attend a coaches' meeting where conference awards for players were decided.

- Basketballs had been lost after practice.

- Hollinger was inconsistent in disciplining players.

- Team execution was inconsistent throughout the season.

- Hollinger encouraged players to concentrate on only basketball.

- Hollinger prepared an unfavorable evaluation of Assistant Coach Capelli's performance.

- Differences in philosophy between Hollinger and the administration were escalated to the community.

Coach Hollinger was shocked to read each of the aforementioned charges and, in each instance, believed he could rebut their substance and validity. Hollinger viewed the charges as myths and half-truths fabricated by some players' parents, who believed their kid should be given more playing time, as well as jealous coaches who secretly wanted his job.

## THE FACT-FINDING HEARING

Pursuant to Coach Hollinger's request, Superintendent Pat Sims agreed to convene a "fact-finding" hearing on the matter. Superintendent Sims asked Marcia Lubara, a dispute resolution specialist from Tempe, to conduct the hearing and render an advisory opinion to her regarding whether Dave Hollinger should be prohibited from applying for the coaching job and, if so, how long the prohibition should stay in effect.

At the outset of the hearing, Lubara set forth three issues for her determination and recommendation:

- Was Hollinger entitled to automatically continue from year to year as head basketball coach?

- Was DVUSD obligated to establish that there was just cause not to automatically continue Hollinger as head basketball coach and, if so, what is the appropriate remedy?

- Whether DVUSD violated the Collective Bargaining Agreement (CBA) when it denied Dave Hollinger the right to apply and be considered for a vacant head basketball coaching position.

At the beginning of the hearing, the district's legal counsel, Peter Lassen, set forth the district's official view of the matter: Lassen contended that extra duty positions, including coaching assignments, are one-year appointments made at the discretion of DVUSD administrators. Lassen explained that there is no tenure associated with these positions nor is there any justified expectation to continued employment beyond the one-year contractual term. Accordingly, the non-renewal of Hollinger for the head basketball coaching position for the 1997–98 school year was proper. Furthermore, the position of coach is not afforded the same due process rights as that of a certified teacher. Therefore, Hollinger was not entitled to remain as coach and the district did not have to justify its reasons for prohibiting Hollinger from reapplying for the coaching job in the future.

However, fact-finder Lubara reminded everyone at the hearing that the issue of whether DVUSD had just cause to terminate Hollinger's coaching position is only relevant if Hollinger had tenure or a property right as a coach. In other words, Lubara clarified her position—Hollinger is entitled to due process rights as a coach only if the DVUSD accorded these rights through its personnel policies or negotiated said due process rights through collective negotiations with DVEA.

Tommy Mack, assistant principal and athletic director at DVHS, testified that he understood that coaches were given a one-year contract upon the recommendation of the athletic director to the principal. Mack stated that his practice was to evaluate all coaches at DVHS as the athletic director and that he utilized a standard form for this purpose. Mack testified that he distributed a copy of the Athletic Handbook to all coaches on October 6, 1993; the aforementioned handbook indicated that the coaching contract is for a one-year period of time.

Wayne Kimball testified that as athletic director he had provided all coaches with a copy of the Athletic Handbook, which stated that "all coaching assignments are one-year appointments" with a renewal option at the discretion of the principal. Kimball said that the athletic director was subsequently given an advisory role in the decision-making process. Kimball added that the principal's authority to decide upon renewal of coaching contracts was consistently followed in practice as well. Kimball stated that he used a form when evaluating coaches and this evaluation was placed in the coach's personnel file and reviewed by the principal when making the renewal decision. Kimball disagreed with those coaches who signed an affidavit stating that they considered their coaching positions to be automatically renewed unless they resigned or received a poor performance evaluation.

Hollinger testified that his coaching or addenda contract was for $2,400 each basketball season and that he also directed a basketball program in the summer, which netted approximately $1,500. Hollinger stated that past practice was to circulate a memo to coaches at the end of the year in order to determine if the coach wished to have her or his contract renewed. Hollinger admitted that he received the Athletic Handbook during 1993–94 year, but not in subsequent seasons. Specifically, Hollinger stated that he did not receive the Athletic Handbook in 1994–95, nor did he see Mack's accompanying memo of October 6, 1993.

Donald Kline, a DVHS faculty member and assistant coach during 1992–93, testified that he was unaware that the Athletic Handbook existed during his service as coach. Kline also indicated that past practice was to allow coaches either to resign or be "due processed" out of a coaching position.

Kline stated that a coaching "vacancy" occurs either through resignation or when one is evaluated out.

Molly France, girls basketball coach for nine years at DVHS, stated that coaches were allowed to continue in their coaching positions unless they were evaluated out of them.

Robert Ioccoca, an elementary school teacher and assistant baseball coach, testified that coaches were hired by the principal but were removed only by resignation or by being evaluated out.

Betty Kim stated that she understood that coaches would be terminated only by resignation or by evaluation criteria to be determined ahead of time. Kim stated that all coaching positions the previous year were made "at will," which was a radical departure from past practice, when coaches were given reasons for removal prior to a nonrenewal decision by the principal. Kim testified that the 1993–96 CBA indicates that coaching positions are "at will" in nature.

Sandra Stevens, member of DVEA's negotiating team, testified that she believed coaches could be terminated only through voluntary resignation or following an evaluation process.

Dave Hollinger stated that the head basketball coach for 1996–97 resigned in November after being hired in October, and Hollinger had intended to immediately apply for the vacant position. However, Hollinger was not permitted to apply for the job. Betty Kim testified that she sent a letter of protest to Dr. Sims on November 16, 1996, because the district was recruiting for a new basketball coach even though Hollinger was obviously well qualified for the position. Sandra Stevens stated that Tommy Mack refused to meet with her on November 10 and 11 regarding his refusal to consider Hollinger's application for head basketball coach. Stevens stated that Dr. Bob James, associate superintendent for curriculum and development and acting superintendent, also refused to allow Hollinger to reapply for the position of head basketball coach. (James stated that Hollinger could not be rehired for a position from which he had just been terminated, but could apply for a similar position that had become available at Barry Goldwater High School.) Stevens testified that the DVUSD's refusal to consider Hollinger's application constituted a *reprisal* as prohibited by a provision of the 1993–96 CBA.

Hearing Officer and fact-finder Lubara concluded the hearing and prepared to make her reommendation to Superintendent Sims.

## DISCUSSION

1.  Did the Deer Valley Unified School District act properly in its decision to terminate Coach Hollinger's employment as head boys basketball coach?

2.  Did the district's action of not considering Coach Hollinger's application for the vacant position violate its own personnel policies and practices?

3.  If you were Hearing Officer Lubara, what would you recommend to Superintendent Sims?

# 2

## PROMOTION

# Tom Collins Doesn't Mix Well

*Arizona was the final state in the union to recognize the third Monday in January as a national holiday in commemoration of the birth date of Dr. Martin Luther King, Jr. For years, Arizona resisted national pressure to join the rest of the country. Finally, in order to avoid losing conventions and national sporting events, Arizona relented and recognized Reverend Dr. Martin Luther King, Jr., Day.*

Tom Collins had been a full-time employee of the Phoenix Union High School District (PUHSD) since he was first hired as a custodian on December 6, 1987. Collins worked in that position for approximately two and one-half years prior to transferring to the paint shop. With performance reviews that were above expectations, Collins was subsequently hired as an apprentice painter and promoted to positions of journeyman painter and lead painter during the following six years. From October 16 until November 20, 1996, he was temporarily upgraded to the position of chief painter when the position became vacant and the district carried out the search process for filling it. On November 20, Collins and three other applicants were verbally informed that they had not been selected for the position of chief painter. Instead, Pete Farias, an employee with less education, seniority, and experience, was given the position.

Collins was extremely upset with the selection of Farias, particularly following his own performance in the position as an upgrade. Collins suspected, but without hard evidence, that his supervisor, James Langdon, had sabotaged the process. Collins suspected that Langdon was prejudiced against him as the only African American employee in the shop. Collins also suspected that the fact that he wasn't a "socializer" and didn't mix with the other employees had been held against him. More substantial to his case, Collins and the grievance committee of the Phoenix Union High School District Classified Employees Association (PUHSD-CEA) believed that the district had violated two key provisions of its own Classified Employees Association (CEA) Handbook in the hiring process.

Thus, when all attempts to resolve his complaint failed, Tom Collins filed a grievance against the district on January 9, 1997. The issue articulated in the grievance was whether the district violated the CEA Handbook when it promoted Pete Farias to the position of chief painter, while it denied promotion into the same position to Collins. In his grievance, Tom Collins cited the following relevant portions of the district's CEA Handbook:

### Filling Vacancies in Permanent Positions (Section 21)

When a vacant or permanent position is identified and is to be filled, a personnel action sheet listing the essential information concerning the vacancy will be prepared by the employee relations office and sent to each unit. The personnel action sheet will be posted immediately on the designated bulletin board at each location. The next daily bulletin distributed within each school after the receipt of the notice will include the listing of vacancies. Interested applicants must observe the deadline for making application, which will be five (5) days. Temporary position vacancies will not be advertised. Summer positions will be advertised.

Application must be made for each job advertised. There will be no carryover. Applications are to be made in writing to the employee relations office with a copy to the appropriate administrative supervisor.

All permanent employees of the district who are qualified in accord with job description requirements and who apply for the advertised position prior to the closing date will be scheduled for an interview.

1. As timely as possible after the closing date to make application, the employee relations office will advise the appropriate administrative supervisor of the applicants to be scheduled for an interview.
2. The administrative supervisor will contact each district applicant and schedule an interview.

Selection will be made from among the applications by the appropriate administrator/supervisor.

District applicants who were interviewed for the position will be notified by memorandum when the selection is made.

### Promotion to Higher Classification (Section 42)

Whenever promotions are made to higher classifications, selections will be made, first, on the employee's experience, training, and knowledge in relation to the position requirement; and, second, on the employee's seniority. The district reserves the right to select the best person for the position, regardless of whether this person is an employee of the district.

The grievance filed by Collins provided space for both the grievant's position and the remedy sought, as well as the official response by the district. The divergent positions of both parties were stated as follows.

## POSITION OF THE ASSOCIATION

In order to have filled the position of chief painter by promotion, the district should be compelled to comply with the CEA Handbook. The district failed to comply with the CEA Handbook, which is written in clear and unambiguous language. This CEA Handbook obligates the district to make the selection for promotion according to an employee's experience, training, and knowledge in relation to the position requirements. In the instant case, the interviewing committee members did not make the selection according to the established criteria and therefore violated the CEA Handbook. In addition, there are certain procedural requirements that the district is obligated to comply with when filling vacancies in permanent positions, such as hiring the applicant with the most education and experience. Specifically, the district failed to comply with paragraph E of said section, which obligates the district to notify all district applicants by memorandum when the selection for promotion is made. The district did not do this and therefore failed to follow the Handbook's language on this matter. For these reasons the association believes that the grievance should be upheld.

## THE DISTRICT'S POSITION

All required procedures contained in the CEA Handbook were followed in the filling of the chief painter position. Specifically, the district posted the vacancy notice on October 25, 1996, accepted applications through the closing date, screened the applicants, and determined those eligible for an interview; it interviewed the candidates on November 15, 1996, made a selection from among those candidates, and notified the applicants on November 17, 1996, of the selection.

There are no provisions contained in the CEA Handbook requiring that any information supplied by candidates for a position be provided to the interviewers. The district is not required to submit the employee's PR-14 (which asks the applicant to explain how he or she meets the job description qualifications) to the interviewers. Furthermore, there are no provisions in the CEA Handbook requiring that job descriptions be used by interviewers to determine the qualifications of candidates. Perhaps most importantly, the 1996–97 CEA Handbook grants the district the ultimate right to select "the best person" for the position. In other words, regardless of any other considerations, the district retains the right to make the final selection.

In order to prepare its case for the arbitration hearing, the association assigned Charles Nighthorse to represent

Collins. Nighthorse knew that he could not convince the arbitrator with allegations of racial discrimination or retaliation because of Collins' reluctance to mix with other employees. Nighthorse planned to interview witnesses and collect hard evidence during the discovery phase of hearing preparation. Nighthorse conducted several interviews with potential witnesses over the next several weeks and uncovered the following information:

• *Mary Koutis* informed Nighthorse that she has been the chief negotiator for the association during the past two years and involved with collective bargaining with the district during the last ten years. She stated that the CEA Handbook set forth two criteria that must be followed when promoting bargaining unit employees. First, each employee's experience, training, and knowledge in relation to the position requirements are considered. Secondly, when two applicants are roughly equal on the first criterion, seniority is considered. Koutis indicated to Nighthorse that the intent of the handbook was to select the most qualified person for the job, with consideration given to both formal and informal training.

Mary Koutis stated that all applicants are required to complete a PR-14. Koutis testified that in order for Pete Farias to be promoted, his qualifications would have to have been greater than those of Tom Collins; had Collins and Farias both had roughly equal qualifications, the one with greater seniority should have prevailed. Koutis was prepared to testify that Collins had both better qualifications and more seniority than Farias.

• *Jim Badar,* an employment specialist in human resources, informed Nighthorse that a Seniority Listing of Classified Personnel, Support Services Schedule, dated January 30, 1989, lists the hire date of Pete Farias as March 3, 1988, and the hire date of Tom Collins as December 6, 1987.

• *Martha Feria* stated that she has extensive experience as an officer of CEA and on the negotiating team. Feria informed Nighthorse that she was on the negotiating team in 1995 when the association proposed to the district that the language be changed so that management rights to hire whomever they wanted be stricken. However, Feria stated that the district persuaded them not to change the phrase. Feria admitted that the management rights language had been a part of the CEA Handbook as far back as 1974–75.

• *Tom Collins* told Nighthorse that, prior to being employed by the district, he became certified as a qualified journeyman painter, which included 24 hours of general college credit and 26 college hours of journeyman training. Collins indicated on his PR-14 for chief painter that he had attended Maricopa Technical College for three years and had completed the painter's apprenticeship program. Collins also indicated on the PR-14 that he had worked as a painter for 17 years, 14 of which were with PUHSD. Collins stated that he has worked with Pete Farias and initially helped train him as a painter.

• *Kathleen De La Cruz* stated that she was prepared to testify that she has selected candidates for many classified positions during her years as a district administrator. De La Cruz stated that she assumes that all candidates referred by the district personnel office are qualified and that she does not consider seniority as a hiring factor among district employees. De La Cruz testified that she attempts to match applicant skills to job requirements and that she will occasionally look at personnel files of district applicants.

• *Roger Haliburton,* director of classified services for approximately 22 years, informed Nighthorse that he personally has written about 80 percent of the CEA Handbook. Haliburton stated that an employee's experience, training, and knowledge are paramount considerations in promotional decisions and that seniority is a secondary consideration. Haliburton said, however, that the district reserves the right to select whomever it feels is best for the position. Roger Haliburton indicated that each job applicant is required to complete a PR-14 form in order to show how he or she qualifies for a particular job. This form is then reviewed by the district office for the sole purpose of determining whether one meets the job qualifications. Haliburton stated that the PR-14 is not routinely supplied to the interviewers. Haliburton indicated that sometimes an interviewer would request to review the PR-14 and the employee's personnel file, but not usually. Haliburton was not on the interviewing panel for the chief painter position and has no personal knowledge of how the PR-14 forms were used by interviewers, if at all.

• *Howard Green,* maintenance coordinator, indicated to Nighthorse that he chaired the interview process that had been used for the selection of chief painter. Green stated that each of the candidates interviewed was asked the same ten questions, and each was rated on a score sheet up to a maximum of five points per answer. The candidate with the highest cumulative score was selected for the position. Green indicated "that he did not remember whether the interviewing committee looked at the PR-14s of either Farias or Collins and that the committee believed Farias had more work experience than Collins." Green also stated that candidates were asked questions concerning their job experience and knowledge. Howard Green admitted that he called the five candidates together subsequently and informed them that he had bad new for Collins and the other three and good news for Farias; he then told them that Farias had received the promotion. Green also confirmed that he asked Henry Morales (another applicant) if he felt Collins would cause trouble because of Farias's selection. Howard Green testified that he was unsure of how much college education Farias had and that Farias received the highest rating score. Collins was rated second highest but there was supposedly a wide gap between them. Green also stated that he was aware that Farias had never worked for PUHSD as a lead painter or chief painter.

• *Henry Morales,* who also was interviewed for the position of chief painter, testified that Jim Langdon, who was on the interviewing committee, told him on October 31, 1996, that Tom Collins would not be selected for the chief painter position if Langdon had anything to do about it. Jim Langdon stated that he did not have a discussion with Morales prior to the interview and denied ever making said statement to Morales.

## DISCUSSION

1.   What are the strongest points that Nighthorse has to use in planning his case? Where is his case weakest?

2.    What safeguards should the district have taken to pre-
      serve the legitimacy of the promotion process in this
      matter?

3.    If you were the district superintendent, would you take
      the case to arbitration or would you attempt to reach a
      settlement?

# 3

## JOB EVALUATION

# Some Counselors Are More Equal Than Others

*What kind of funny farm are they running here anyway? We all hold the same job title and job specifications. We're all basically social workers and yet, just because we work within different departments in state government, they want to pay us different wages. It doesn't make sense. Either treat the jobs equally or change the job titles, but don't insult our intelligence!*

Rose Paddock was hopping mad! Rose, as a part of her studies toward a master of public administration degree, recently completed an introductory course in human resources management that included an overview of job evaluation principles and practices in public sector organizations. For example, Rose understood that position classifiers traditionally tried to apply such principles as, "classify the position, not the person" and "like positions grouped in the same classification." Yet Rose, a career state employee, was surprised to learn how frequently objective "theory" that she learned in textbooks was not practiced by her employer, the state of New Mexico. The same job title that Rose held, "employment counselor," had been reclassified upward in the state's Department of Labor, while the same job title and position in the state's Human Services Department (HSD) had been denied reclassification and was kept in the same classification range. Both positions had the same job duties, responsibilities, and qualifications.

How could the same job title and job specification for employment counselor be classified differently by an employer, simply because the employees worked in two different state departments? It reminded Rose of the classic line from George Orwell's futuristic *Animal Farm* wherein "some animals were more equal than others." Nor was Rose the only employment counselor in HSD who was agitated and demanded a reassessment of classification. So, quite naturally Rose and her coworkers decided to talk to their union about the way they were being treated.

## THE UNION'S POSITION

The union was only too willing to take up the cause it believed had been created by the state. Rose and her 35 coworkers, who were employment counselors within HSD's Income Support Division (ISD), were represented by the American Federation of State, County, and Municipal Employees (AFSCME), Local #2839. The employment counselor's job included occupational counseling of welfare clients who are searching for work. These positions were classified as a grade 18 and involved very similar job duties and responsibilities as employment counselor (EC) in the State Department of Labor (DOL). In November 1996, following a job evaluation study by the State Personnel Office, the ECs in DOL were reclassified upward to a grade 19, which has a grade cap of $15.20 per hour, compared to a cap of $13.40 per hour for grade 18.

By contrast, in January 1994, a reclassification study was initiated for ECs in HSD, but it was subsequently denied by the State Department of Finance and Administration (DFA) because of a lack of sufficient funds within the HSD budget. The union contended that the state's failure to automatically upgrade ECs at HSD following the DOL upgrade was discriminatory because of agency affiliation and a violation of Articles 8 and 12 of the Collective Bargaining Agreement (CBA, see below). The union argued that the employer is the state of New Mexico, not the HSD, and therefore must treat all employees with the same job title equally. If correct, the validity of the reclassification study conducted on ECs in the DOL would apply to all ECs throughout state government, regardless of department and alleged budgetary constraints. The union contended that "discrimination" by departmental affiliation is no less discriminatory than that stemming from racial, ethnic, religious, or gender bias. In fact, many ECs in HSD believed that an underlying reason for the refusal by the state to reclassify their positions could be attributed to the predominance of male ECs in the DOL and the majority of female ECs in the HSD.

## THE DEPARTMENT'S POSITION

The department's position is that, despite the fact that it had attempted to reclassify the ECs in 1994, it was nonetheless bound by certain procedure set forth by the State Personnel Board and controlling legislation that must be followed as agreed to in Articles 14 and 25 of the CBA (see below). Although the ECs' reclassification in DOL was successful, HSD was prohibited from upgrading its ECs in 1994 by the Department of Finance and Administration (DFA) because of inadequate funds in its budget. The department also asserted that neither the union nor the ECs ever grieved their reclassification denial in 1994; neither did they initiate a request for reclassification in 1997. Finally, management asserted that the union and the ECs in HSD had no standing to claim discrimination because they never "went through the appropriate channels" to request a job evaluation study in 1997.

## THE INTERACTION

Both union and management argued that the other side had violated the CBA. Specifically, the union charged that management's violation occurred in November 1996 when, in upgrading the position of employment counselor, the State Personnel Office failed to include ECs within the HSD in the pay increase retroactive to January 1996. The union wanted no less a remedy than reclassification and complete retroactive pay.

In January 1994, the HSD initiated a classification

study for its employment counselor positions; this was the first in a series of steps that the State Personnel Office required to conduct a job evaluation study. As part of this study, questionnaires were circulated among incumbent employees and their supervisors in which they were asked questions regarding job duties, responsibilities, and tasks, as well as incumbent knowledge, skills, and abilities. In a few instances, the job evaluators also conducted "desk audits." The second stage of the mandated reclassification process is that the state's DFA must review the department's budget and determine if sufficient funds are allocated to cover requested reclassification upgrades. In October 1995, the reclassification upgrades for ECs were denied, not because the point-factor analysis of job duties and responsibilities did not merit upward reclassification, but because of a lack of funds in the HSD budget. The reclassification study was consequently tabled and the position incumbents did not file a grievance on appeal.

Concurrently in late 1995, the State DOL initiated a classification study of its employment counselors, and on November 16, 1995, the State Personnel Board conditionally approved the reclassification, contingent on DFA certification of funds. In January 1997, the DFA determined that sufficient money for reclassification was available in the DOL budget, and its ECs were subsequently reclassified upward to a grade 19 and given retroactive pay to January 1996.

In April 1997, this action provoked Rose Paddock and her mostly female coworkers in HSD to file a class action grievance, to protest the fact that HSD ECs were not reclassified and given retroactive pay, even though these employees had not requested a new job evaluation study.

In the union's initial grievance and in management's written response, both parties cited the following sections of the CBA as relevant:

## Article 8—New or Altered Classifications

The Employer may establish new job classifications, or abolish, merge, or change existing job classifications of employees covered by this Agreement in accordance with the Personnel Act (Section 10-9-1, *et seq.* NMSA 1978). At the time of such action, the Employer shall identify the employees covered by this Agreement to be included in any new or altered job classification and shall identify the old job classification(s), if any, which in whole or in part are being replaced. Unless it is supervisory, confidential, or managerial, as defined in PEBA Section 4, any new or altered job classification that, in whole or part, replaces a job classification already represented by a signatory Union, shall be included in a bargaining unit of the signatory Unions.

## Article 12—Nondiscrimination

With respect to the terms and conditions of employment, the parties shall not discriminate against any employee covered by this Agreement on the grounds of non-merit factors except as otherwise specifically provided for in this Agreement.

Grievances filed under this Article shall specify in writing the non-merit factor(s) upon which the alleged discrimination has been based and the manner in which the alleged discrimination occurred.

## Article 14—Grievance and Arbitration Procedure

**A.** Grievances must be initiated by speaking with the immediate supervisor promptly, but within seven (7) calendar days, after the grievant or the Union was aware, or reasonably could have become aware, of the incident(s) giving rise to the alleged grievance. Employees are encouraged to discuss and attempt to resolve any problem with their immediate supervisor before filing a formal grievance under the procedure established below.

**B.** Matters previously subject to review by the State Personnel Board shall not be subject to arbitration. However, these matters may be grieved up to and including Step 4 of the Grievance and Arbitration procedure set out in this Article.

## Article 25—Job Classification

### Section Two—Requesting Reclassification

Any employee covered by this agreement who believes that her or his actual job position in the classified service is not assigned to the class that best represents the duties assigned by the Employer may initiate a request for a new position classification assignment through procedures established by the SPB and the Department of Finance and Administration. If the employee's position is subsequently assigned to a different job classification and the employee meets the minimum qualifications for that position, the employee shall be paid the appropriate salary for the new job classification as provided by SPB rules.

---

Both parties have agreed to select an arbitrator to hear their respective positions and render a final and binding decision. The arbitrator has the discretion to rule in favor of either party or craft his or her own decision, but must stay within the language of the CBA, if it is clearly and unambiguously written. When CBA language is unclear or ambiguous, it will be the arbitrator's task to apply appropriate interpretation to the articles cited as having been violated. The arbitrator also cannot modify state law that takes precedence over the CBA.

## DISCUSSION

1.  If you were the union's Grievance Committee, would you recommend pushing this case all the way to arbitration? If you were the HSD cabinet secretary, are there possible compromises you might explore?

2.  To what extent should reclassification requests be handled at the departmental level rather than by a central state agency? How can budgetary and financial costs be considered when making reclassification decisions?

3.  You are the arbitrator; what would your decision be (considering only the facts that have been presented to you)?

# 4

## COMPENSATION

# Paying the
# Tucson Police

*Why do we have to beg for better wages? Why do we have*
*to get on our hands and knees to ask for merit increases*
*every year or a pay plan that was put into effect years ago*
*and agreed to? Where is the appreciation for the men and*
*women who go out day and night to protect life and prop-*
*erty? Citizens do not call a restaurant or a developer or*
*the Copper Bowl when they are being burglarized, beaten,*
*or robbed. They call 911 and ask for police assistance.*
*—Letter to the Tucson mayor*

The city of Tucson's charter mandates "Advisory arbitration
of wage disputes" (Section 2) in a unique process that has
evolved since its initiation in 1971 and is quite apart from
collective bargaining. In fact, wages and employee benefits
cannot be negotiated into a collective bargaining agreement,
by Arizona law. Thus, in Tucson, wage discussions begin with
a "meet and confer" dialog between the mayor and representatives of employee unions. Following discussions, the city's
human resources director, under authority of the mayor and
city council, presents a proposed pay plan in a public hearing
to solicit community input and debate.

    If there is still a dispute raised by the employees, the
mayor appoints an advisory arbitration committee to hear

evidence submitted by both sides regarding the merits of each party's proposal. This panel is composed of a representative of both sides and chaired by a neutral arbitrator. The panel conducts a hearing to hear testimony, consider evidence, and hear arguments regarding the merits of both proposals. It then submits their recommendation in writing to the mayor and city council. The panel can accept either proposal or devise its own recommendation. In turn, the council and mayor may adopt, in whole or in part, the committee's recommendation.

In 1997, the Tucson Police Officers Association (TPOA) and the city reached an impasse over the proposed compensation plan and submitted their dispute to advisory arbitration. The TPOA requested across-the-board pay increases of 6 percent for all 795 officers in the bargaining unit, along with merit step increases and other benefits.

By contrast, the human resources director proposed a compensation plan that created an additional step (Step 10) at the top of the pay scale and full merit pay increases based primarily on performance evaluations. The new pay step would have immediately benefitted the approximately 220 officers who were capped out in Step 9 and ineligible to receive an across-the-board raise. In addition, the merit step increase meant that virtually every other officer, detective, or sergeant would be eligible to receive either a 2.5-percent or 5-percent increase, depending on individual performance evaluations.

Although not specified in the city charter, three of the more commonly accepted criteria for evaluating the merits of pay proposals in public sector impasses include (1) an employer's ability to pay for the raise, (2) comparability with wages paid by other competitive employers, and (3) past practices and history of the parties in negotiations. Each of these criteria was applied by the neutral arbitrator in breaking the impasse between Tucson and its police officers.

## ABILITY TO PAY

The TPOA's position is that the city of Tucson has the ability to allocate budgetary resources for a 6-percent across-the-board pay increase for its sworn police officers. It pointed out that in 1995 the percentage increase in the Tucson area's annual wages among all employers was the fifth highest in the country at 6 percent. The association introduced its analysis of the consumer price index-U to demonstrate that wage increases for the Tucson police officers had not kept pace with estimated price increases since 1989.

Nor did the association accept what it considered to be the city's dire fiscal projections; if the city council could approve $7 million for a solar village, a $600,000 increase for youth programs, $700,000 to Janos Restaurant to stay in the Tucson Museum of Art complex, $116.5 million for new city public works projects, and $73,683 to maintain the Copper Bowl, then TPOA saw no reason why the city couldn't make police raises a higher priority. The union therefore requested a 6-percent across-the-board raise to begin retroactively at the start of the fiscal year.

The TPOA offered four options to the arbitration panel for funding a pay increase. The panel was to choose the option it deemed to be most appropriate:

1. *The panel may declare an "emergency" on the basis that the lack of an adequate wage increase "will result in the deterioration of high standards of law enforcement in Tucson, devastate morale, and jeopardize exemplary performance."* Pursuant to Arizona Revised Statutes (ARS) 42-303, a finding of an emergency would then allow the city to find money from budgetary items other than the police department to fund an increase.

2. *Applying ARS 42-303, the panel may recommend that anticipated excess funds from the police department budget be applied toward the wage increase.* The association argued that there were presently 104 vacancies in the bargaining unit, in terms of authorized versus actual strength, thereby providing an anticipated excess in the police budget of at least $3.12 million (assuming $30,000 per officer for wages and benefits).

3. *The panel may take money from the strategic reserve and apply it toward an increase*, keeping in mind that there will be overages in other budget categories at the end of the fiscal year.

4. *The panel may recommend that the pay increase be deferred until the next fiscal year*; in fact, the city charter implies that any recommendation by the panel could be enacted in the following fiscal year.

The city's position obviously was quite the opposite—it would be financially irresponsible to fund the pay increase of $2.2 million, as proposed by TPOA. The Tucson budget and research director pointed out that the police department already had the largest share of the budget (21.9 percent) and the city was almost broke in 1990, when it set aside an emergency reserve equal to 5 percent of the total budget. Furthermore, the budget director warned that the city faced the prospect of expensive incorporation of suburbs surrounding Tucson, a deteriorating infrastructure, and needed capital improvement projects. He also asserted that selected economic indicators for comparison with the Phoenix area were specious because per capita income, annual earnings, and tax revenues were much lower in Tucson. Finally, the city's budget director asserted that the alleged $7,131,800 difference in the currently adopted budget and the estimated budget would actually make available $166,261 in unrestricted funds.

## COMPARABILITY WITH WAGES PAID BY OTHER EMPLOYERS

Employers consider the marketplace and competition from other employers as factors when setting equitable pay rates. An employer's ability to attract and retain competent employees is determined, in part, by what competitors are willing to pay their employees. Thus, the city of Tucson could possibly compare its wage structure to a mix of employers in either the public or private sectors. Prior to choosing a sample for comparative purposes, an employer should answer two questions: (1) from what sources has it historically attracted entry-level officers, and (2) what is the turnover or loss rate of officers to other employers each year?

The city presented data regarding where applicants to the police department lived at the time of their application: Approximately 80 percent of the applicants for police officer positions listed Tucson as their domicile; 105 were from out of state, and 84 were from other Arizona cities. Fifteen applicants were subsequently hired in October 1995 and 12 applicants were hired in October 1996. The department received 1,086 applications in January 1997, from which it employed 40 officers. Secondly, the turnover rate for the Tucson Police Department's sworn officers was 0.9 percent in 1995–96 and 1.7 percent in 1996–97; these percentages are approximately half of the turnover rate of other city departments. Officer retirement rather than resignation caused virtually all of this turnover. Thus, Tucson would not appear to actively compete with other jurisdictions for officer recruitment, nor do these statistics suggest that Tucson's officers are being lured away by other police departments with higher pay and other incentives.

Three possible samples can be used for comparison of pay and benefits given to police officers: (1) other Arizona cities, including those in the Phoenix valley, (2) a mix of selected police departments within the western United States, and (3) other public- and private-sector employers in the Tucson area. Not surprisingly, depending on which sample is used, Tucson's compensation package appears somewhat better or worse. The following comparative samples are pertinent:

• *Regional Salary Data (1996–97)* of wages paid to police officers in 18 cities selected from the western United States show that Tucson's average salary ($34,848) is 1.33 percent less than the average mid-point ($35,312) and 1 percent less than actual salaries paid. The city decided, upon recommendation of its consultant (Ernst and Young), to compare its salaries to a regional sample in 1996–97 rather than the Arizona sample that it had previously used.

• *Arizona Public Safety Survey (1996–97)* of wages paid to law enforcement personnel in 19 Arizona jurisdictions (cities, counties, university police, and state Public Safety) indicated that Tucson is slightly over 5 percent below the average structure and 8 percent below actual salaries paid.

• *Local Police Officer Market Survey (fiscal year 1996–97)* of wages paid to police officers in the Tucson area (N=8) indicates that police salaries paid by the city of Tucson are higher than other police departments, with the exception of the State Department of Public Safety.

The city offered evidence that the following economic indicators are significantly lower in the Tucson metro area when compared to the Phoenix-Mesa area: (1) per capita personal income (-17.2 percent), (2) annual earnings per worker (-13.0 percent), and (3) actual average salary paid to police officers (-15.3 percent). The union offered a "Wage and Benefit Comparability Survey," for which it had contracted, showing that "contrary to common belief," the Cost of Living Index indicated that "it cost almost the same to live in Tucson as it does in Phoenix."

## PAST HISTORY OF NEGOTIATIONS

As indicated, a third criterion commonly considered by arbitrators when deciding the merits of public sector pay impasses is the past practice and history of the parties in negotiations. The city of Tucson and the TPOA's negotiations ("meet and confer") have produced the outcomes in the accompanying table since 1992–93:

| Year | Date Implemented | Compensation Plan Increases | Step Increases |
|------|------------------|------------------------------|----------------|
| 1992–93 | 9/20/92 | 3.0% | None |
|  | 3/21/93 | 3.0% | None |
| 1993–94 | 6/27/93 | None | None |
| 1994–95 | 6/6/94 | None | Full funding |
| 1995–96 | 6/25/95 | 3.0% | Full funding plus lump sum payment to officers at top pay range (2.5% or 5%) |
| 1996–97 | 6/23/96 | None | Full funding |
| 1997–98 | 6/22/97 | Addition of step 10 | Full funding |

Again, it should be noted that step increases are determined by performance evaluations of individual officers and do not occur automatically. However, only four officers out of 827 had step increases either delayed or denied in 1997–1998.

## DISCUSSION

1. You are the association's representative on the panel. Which are your strongest and weakest arguments for justifying a pay increase?

2. You are the city councilor on the panel. Which are your most persuasive and least persuasive arguments for not granting an across-the-board increase?

3. You are a neutral arbitrator on the panel. What is your recommendation to the mayor and city council?

# 5

## THE FAIR LABOR STANDARDS ACT

# Flexing to
# Avoid Overtime

*Social workers are dedicated professionals who are com-*
*mitted to helping others in need. They certainly don't do*
*their jobs for the money or high status. If they're willing*
*to work long hours in order to visit clients in their homes,*
*why can't the state at least pay them overtime when nec-*
*essary? We're not asking for a lot of overtime pay, but*
*when it's occasionally necessary, why would an employer*
*try to avoid paying a little bit of overtime by forcing social*
*workers to stay home rather than accumulate more than*
*40 hours in a work week?*

## BACKGROUND

John Yellow Dog enjoyed his work with the state of
Wyoming as a social worker; his primary job responsibilities were for ensuring compliance with the state's laws
regarding adoptive and foster care services. Yellow Dog's
job was certainly demanding; he often had to travel great
distances across the state's vast expanses, sometimes in
inclement weather, to conduct home visits with families
who had accepted foster care or adoption placements. It
was not uncommon for him to put in 10- or 12-hour days.
Although based in the state capital, Cheyenne, Yellow Dog

would occasionally make day trips to the Casper and Lander areas to visit clients. When Yellow Dog was initially hired in 1991 as a new social worker, he would sometimes work 60- and 70-hour weeks; and in the process rack up considerable amounts of overtime pay at the mandated time-and-a-half rate.

However, state revenues began to drop in the late 1970s, and by the 1990s, department heads were under intense pressure to find new ways to reduce expenditures. Specifically, the Department of Family Services (DFS) and other departments of Wyoming state government targeted overtime costs as a priority for expenditure reduction. One of the identified techniques was through the implementation of a practice known as "flexing" an employee's work schedule in order to reduce overtime costs. Typically, an employee who worked more than eight consecutive hours per day could be ordered by her or his supervisor to "flex" time by working a correspondingly reduced amount of work hours during the same work week. Thus, an employee who worked 10 hours on Monday might be directed to only work six hours on Tuesday in order not to accumulate more than 40 hours in one work week, and therefore be paid overtime. In effect, the department required an employee to alter work hours during the same work week in lieu of accruing overtime hours.

Because of the restrictions on overtime, Yellow Dog's caseload seemed to increase as he fell further behind. His supervisor, Janice Chen, continued to flex Yellow Dog's work schedule to keep her budget in line. Chen pleaded with Yellow Dog, "Look, John, I understand your problem, but the state can't pay overtime or hire any more social workers in the foreseeable future." Yellow Dog angrily replied, "Doesn't the state realize that there's a larger problem here? We're liable for the safe placement of these children and if I can't do my job adequately, I'm personally liable. Social workers in Kentucky and New Mexico have faced criminal charges for not being able to properly perform their jobs!" Chen knew that Yellow Dog's point was well founded but her hands were tied. Yellow Dog decided that ethically he could no longer wait for the caseload situation to worsen; he paid a visit to the president of the local state employees association, Chris Custer.

Chris Custer, also a licensed social worker, had been

looking for a test case on flexing to submit to arbitration as a means of forcing the state to either hire more social workers or pay overtime so that existing social workers could adequately take care of their caseloads. After all, Custer reasoned, that had been one of the original purposes of the Fair Labor Standards Act (FLSA) when it was passed in 1938—to use the threat of overtime as an incentive for employers to hire additional workers.

Custer and Yellow Dog agreed to start by reviewing their case; they would objectively go over all pertinent statutes, personnel rules, and regulations, as well as provisions of the Collective Bargaining Agreement (CBA). What they discovered was both heartening and disappointing. The following documentation was compiled:

## The Collective Bargaining Agreement

- *Article 8.1. Work week–work day.* A normal work week shall be forty (40) hours per week, eight (8) consecutive hours per day, five (5) consecutive days per week, followed by two (2) consecutive days off. The unpaid meal period shall not be considered hours worked. Depending on the needs of a unit of the department, the secretary may deviate from the normal work week.

- *Article 9. Overtime.* No employee shall be required to work in excess of 40 hours a week unless specifically authorized by her or his supervisor for overtime compensation in accordance with the Fair Labor Standards Act and State Personnel Board Rules.

- *Article 9.2. Non-FLSA Bargaining Unit Employees.* Employees in the bargaining unit not covered by the FLSA, who are authorized and required to work in excess of 40 hours in a work week, shall be compensated for such excess hours at their straight time hourly rate in pay or compensatory time. This will be at the employee's option to the extent that budgeted funds are available in the appropriate line item. Employees who are required to work on a day that is observed as a holiday shall be compensated at two-and-one-half times the hourly rate, i.e., their regular rate plus one-and-one-half times that hourly rate. Such compensation may be in pay or in compensatory time.

• *Article 14.2. Consistency of Policies.* Any rules, policies, or practices instituted by management shall be consistent with department rules and directives.

---

## State Personnel Board Rules and Regulations (January 2, 1993)

*Rule 6.9.I. Overtime.* Agencies shall not change the normal work week to avoid payment of overtime.

---

Following a review of the documentation, Yellow Dog and Custer decided that their case was sufficiently strong to pursue an arbitration grievance. Yellow Dog and Custer discussed the pros and cons before deciding that their position would be that State Personnel Board (SPB) Rule 6.9.I is clear and unambiguous; it must be accurately interpreted to prohibit the state from changing the normal work week for the purpose of avoiding payment of overtime to employees. They decided to argue that SPB Rule 6.9.I must also be interpreted in light of the CBA, and regardless of what might be stated in the FLSA. Their case should focus on a demand that the department cease and desist with the practice of altering the work week in order to avoid payment of overtime.

Yellow Dog and Custer knew that the department's position could only be that it has *adjusted* work hours rather than *modified* the work week in order to avoid overtime payments. Workplace practice has been to consider overtime as hours worked in excess of 40 hours per week, not in excess of eight hours each day. This was the accepted practice followed by both union and management in successive CBAs, in the FLSA, and by the director of the SPB. Furthermore, the department's contention is that work adjustment constitutes a residual right of management and a past practice accepted by the State Employees Association.

As anticipated by Yellow Dog and Custer, management employees rejected their arguments and the issue was submitted to an impartial arbitrator for a binding resolution. As required by the arbitrator, the parties met in a pre-hearing conference together and formulated the issue to be resolved in arbitration as follows:

Does the Department have the right to adjust hours within the 40-hour work week in order to limit hours worked to no more than 40 hours each work week and thus avoid having to pay overtime?

Yellow Dog and the association sought as remedy that the department cease its practice of adjusting hours in order to avoid paying overtime. Furthermore, Yellow Dog agreed not to request payment for any overtime denied him by the department's past practice.

The parties selected T. Zane Reeves as impartial arbitrator from a list of potential arbitrators supplied by the Federal Mediation and Conciliation Service. Reeves convened a hearing on January 21, 1994, in Cheyenne, in the Income Support Division conference room in the DFS. Yellow Dog was present and represented by Custer. Mark Katzmann, DFS legal counsel, and Barbara Rowe, DFS labor relations specialist, represented the department.

Prior to beginning the hearing, management moved to prohibit the arbitrator from making any ruling based on state statutes because they were outside the arbitrator's jurisdiction. Katzmann argued that an arbitrator only had authority to interpret a dispute arising from a collective bargaining agreement. Arbitrator Reeves ruled that although rules of an administrative agency such as the SPB are not arbitrable in isolation by an impartial arbitrator, a particular rule that clarifies the meaning of a specific provision of the CBA may be considered for interpretive purposes by the arbitrator. Thus, the SPB's Rule 6.9.I is a general prohibition against changing the "normal work week" in order to avoid paying overtime. This rule was deemed pertinent by the arbitrator in understanding the context of Article 8.1, which allowed the department to change a normal work week according to unspecified "needs of a unit."

## THE ARBITRATOR'S DECISION

Following a day of hearing testimony and admitting exhibits, the arbitrator issued an award that rejected the claims by Yellow Dog and Custer. The arbitrator cited the following conclusions in his award:

- A "normal" work week is clearly defined as a 40-hour week, eight consecutive hours per day with one unpaid hour off for lunch, followed by two days off. The CBA (Article 8.1) permits the department secretary to deviate from the normal work week, "depending on the needs of a unit of the Department"; this phrase is unclear in its proposed application but the actual effect is to allow supervisors to make "temporary alterations in an employee's schedule within the same work week in order to void overtime liability."

- The association failed to demonstrate that the department violated its CBA with the union. Language in the CBA did not change in successive CBAs, and supervisors have flexed employee schedules within the normal 40-hour work week for many years. It is a practice that was unchallenged by the union in a context of unclear language in the CBA and SPB Rules. To charge that the department violated its CBA with the union by engaging in a long-standing practice that was accepted by both parties would not seem logical.

- Clearly, the SPB has the authority to issue a written interpretation of Rule 6.9.I if it chooses to do so; the board could have also overturned the State Personnel Office (SPO) director's verbal interpretation of the same rule at any time. The parties might also renegotiate the flexing of work hours in a CBA or agree in a letter of understanding to the current contract that flexing within a 40-hour week is prohibited. Until one of these options is taken, the union cannot reasonably demand that management rescind a long-standing workplace practice that initially evolved from vague language in the CBA.

- Management generally retains its right to manage unless it voluntarily limits its right by some specific provision of the CBA. The efficient management of work is a management right and is so noted in Article 5 of the CBA. Nowhere else in the CBA does management limit its right to schedule employee work hours except to indicate that it will not alter the "normal 40-hour work week." It remains a managerial prerogative to determine daily work schedules and assignments unless otherwise stated in the CBA or by the SPB.

# DISCUSSION

1. To what extent do you agree with the case as presented and understood by John Yellow Dog and Chris Custer?

2. How would you recommend that management in the Department of Family Services handle the over-time/staffing dilemma?

3. Do you recommend that the overtime policy be redefined as any hours worked in excess of eight hours in a day?

# 6

## EMPLOYEE BENEFITS

# No More
# Nittany Lions

*There's nothing fancy about the football uniforms of Pennsylvania State University; there are no insignia on the helmets or flashy trim on the jerseys and pants—just straight and simple. Despite the lack of glamour, they have one of the most successful football programs in the United States and probably the game's most popular coach. Not coincidentally, Penn State has one of the highest graduation rates of football players in the country. Maybe that's a factor in the sold-out home games every fall. No doubt about it—the Nittany Lions of Penn State have some of the most loyal and enthusiastic fans anywhere.*

Abner Hamm was very upset; he had worked as security supervisor for almost 20 years at one of the country's most prominent teaching hospitals, Penn State's Milton S. Hershey Medical Center (HMC). Hamm, who was a third-generation employee of Penn State, had just learned that HMC and the Geisinger Health System (GHS) would be merging, effective January 17, 1997. On July 1, the Penn State GHS would become a reality, pairing two entities that were originally established by philanthropic trusts from Milton S. Hershey and Abigail Geisinger. As a result of the merger, the 6,070 employees at HMC who were Penn State employees prior to July 1 would no longer wear

Penn State identification badges. Abner Hamm and many of his coworkers felt the merger would bring in a new management culture that didn't understand what it meant to be a part of Penn State, nor did it appreciate the pride of working at one of North America's finest universities and best collegiate football programs.

## PENNSYLVANIA STATE UNIVERSITY AND THE HERSHEY MEDICAL CENTER

The Pennsylvania State University was chartered in 1855 as the Farmers' High School, a pioneer institution established to provide higher education for all social classes. Renamed the Agricultural College of Pennsylvania in 1862, it became a land-grant college in 1863; the Pennsylvania State University designation was adopted in 1953. Today, the Penn State system embodies 24 campuses, more than 72,000 students, and a full-time faculty and staff 13,500 members strong. Penn State draws its income from a number of major sources, including student-generated tuition and fees, restricted funds, state appropriations, and auxiliary enterprises. Tuition and fees constitute the largest single source of Penn State's total operating budget. In fiscal year 1996–97, that proportion was equal to 27.2 percent. Restricted funds (research grants, contracts, and philanthropic gifts from government and private sources) amounted to 18.4 percent of the budget, and state appropriations accounted for 16.8 percent, or roughly one-sixth. Auxiliary enterprises (i.e., the Nittany Lion Inn, Intercollegiate Athletics, and Housing and Food Services) are completely self-supporting activities and contributed 15.4 percent to the budget. Other sources such as HMC and federal agriculture grants provided the balance of the total operating budget of $1.7 billion for 1996–97.

Although Penn State is the largest postsecondary educational institution in the commonwealth of Pennsylvania, the moneys Pennsylvania appropriates for the university from state coffers are relatively minimal. Penn State owes its public character primarily to its designation as the commonwealth's only land-grant university. It is neither owned nor operated by the state: Penn State is separately incorporated, with an independent board of trustees. The university is "an instrumentality of the Commonwealth" and is described as a "state-related" university, as are the University of Pittsburgh, Temple University, and Lincoln University.

Though their proportion relative to other funding sources has declined over the past 30 years, state appropriations remain vital to Penn State's operations. In fiscal year 1996–97, state dollars comprised 34.9 percent of the university's general funds budget, facilitating efforts that run the gamut from teaching and research to operations and maintenance. Not unlike other organizations that receive taxpayer dollars, Penn State must comply with procurement rules when spending those dollars. In this sense, much of the university's flexibility is contingent to a great extent on its other sources of income, as described above, including endowments and grants. Although it is similarly categorized, Penn State receives a smaller appropriation per full-time equivalent student than other state-owned or state-related universities in the commonwealth. Moreover, Pennsylvania ranks 47th in the nation in per capita spending on public higher education.

Founded in 1963 through a gift from the Milton S. Hershey Trust, the HMC encompasses Penn State's College of Medicine, University Hospital, and Children's Hospital. More than 6,000 employees and 500 students support the HMC's mission: During fiscal year 1995–96, university hospitals admitted nearly 20,800 inpatients and administered care to more than 356,000 outpatients and 25,600 emergency-service patients. The 504-bed university hospitals serve as referral centers for patients sent by their own physicians in communities throughout Pennsylvania as well as primary care providers for residents of Hershey, Harrisburg, and the surrounding area. Moreover, they function as settings for educational and research programs unmatched in the region.

## PENN STATE AND HMC EMPLOYEE COMPENSATION PACKAGES

Because HMC was a Pennsylvania State University campus in its entirety prior to July 1, 1997, all Hershey employees worked for Penn State. The university is reputed to be a competitive employer; surveys indicate that Penn State faculty earned upwards of 7 percent more than the national average salary of full-time faculty members at public four-year doctoral institutions in 1995–96. The merger applied to patient care services and operations of HMC. Penn State retained ownership of the HMC facilities, as well as ownership and operation of the College of Medicine. In short, only those employees who were affiliated strictly with the College of Medicine would continue to be employed by Penn State. All other HMC employees were moved to the Penn State Geisinger Health System's payroll. Because the vast majority of HMC physicians are faculty of the Penn State College of Medicine, and remain Penn State employees, their benefits were unaffected by the merger.

With regard to Penn State staff compensation, the staff pay structure took into consideration internal relationships university-wide, as well as competitiveness in the external marketplace where the university recruits for employees. The pay structure had 22 grade levels; each grade contains a variety of jobs. Although jobs may differ, the value of the work in a given grade was very similar, and each grade level had a salary range that represented the pay opportunity for each individual employee whose job is assigned that grade level.

Penn State staff benefits were comprehensive and included traditional provisions such as life insurance and health care as well as nontraditional perquisites such as educational privileges and the ability to legitimately use sick leave to care for an ailing family member. University employees could choose from three life insurance options and several health care programs to satisfy their life and health insurance needs. They were also eligible to select and participate in a tax-deferred annuity program, as provided by Section 403(b) of the Internal Revenue Code.

At most locations in the Penn State system, December 25 and five additional days between/around it and December 31 (depending on which day of the week December 25 falls) are university holidays. Because of the necessary operation of the HMC, the five additional holidays granted in December to other regular university employees were included in the annual accumulation of paid time off (PTO), as established in HMC's PTO/CAT (combined annual time) program prior to July 1, 1997. The PTO/CAT program also provided HMC staff with three weeks of vacation time per year during the first ten years of regular employment, and four weeks from the beginning of the eleventh year and thereafter. University staff members accrue one day (eight hours) of sick leave with pay for each calendar month, and are permitted to charge absences as sick leave when they are unable to perform their duties because of illness or injury, when the employee requires time off for a routine appointment with a physician, dentist, or optometrist, or when he or she requires time off to care for a sick family member. Penn State's policy regarding maternity leave, family care, sickness, and the like (issues covered under the federal Family and Medical Leave Act [FMLA] of 1993) is more generous than FMLA. Other circumstances under which Penn State employees may receive paid time off include a death in the family, involuntary jury service, and volunteer firefighting.

The retirement programs in which staff members may select to participate constitute one of the most attractive benefits associated with employment by Penn State. Employees are eligible to contribute either to the Pennsylvania State Employees' Retirement System (SERS) or the Teachers Insurance and Annuity Association/College Retirement Equities Fund (TIAA-CREF). Faculty and staff contribute 5 percent of their annual salary to either plan. The amount the university contributes to SERS is determined each year by legislative action; in 1997 it contributed 9.29 percent of annual salary to TIAA-CREF. In summary, SERS enables the employee to increase his or her pension, and provides a fixed, formula-based benefit. TIAA-CREF offers immediate vesting, flexibility in vesting contributions, and, in many cases, the ability to transfer from one institution to another.

## NO MORE NITTANY LIONS

Not unlike many postsecondary educational employers, Pennsylvania State University grants educational privileges to regular (and *retired*) staff members and their dependents (spouse and unmarried children, including adopted children and stepchildren). Eligible employees, retirees, and dependents may, upon application by the staff member, receive tuition grant-in-aid for 75 percent of the tuition charge for a maximum of 16 credits in an academic year. Educational privileges are, not surprisingly, one of the most prized components of the overall Penn State compensation package. Thus, thousands of employees at Penn State and the HMC were able to provide for their children's education without having to save a small fortune in the process. Both Abner Hamm's brother and sister had been able to graduate from Penn State because their father had worked at Penn State. Up until the announcement of the Geisinger merger, Abner assumed that his twin 12-year-old daughters, Meagan and Kayce, would also attend one of the Penn State campuses.

The university imparted many other perks to staff members and their families, not the least of which (for Nittany Lion fans, anyway) was the opportunity to purchase season football tickets at a reduced rate. Here in central Pennsylvania, football aficionados could revel in the spirit of tailgate parties and a nationally ranked football program led by their beloved Coach Joe Paterno. Abner and his family faithfully attended home games at Beaver Stadium in Happy Valley; after the merger, paying the full cost of football tickets would make them too expensive.

In addition, recreational and fitness facilities were available free of charge to Penn State employees and their dependents. Many employee-development initiatives and programs promoting health conscientiousness were created as well. Child-care facilities were conveniently located on many campuses within the Penn State system and very reasonably priced. In addition to all these tangible benefits, it is important to mention the intangible remuneration employees enjoyed as members of a highly regarded institution of higher education—the spirit, camaraderie, and personal fulfillment inherent in working for Pennsylvania State University.

## GEISINGER TAKES OVER

Shortly after the turn of the century, Abigail Geisinger, an 85-year-old widow, decided to build a regional health care system. She had the financial support of some Danville, Pennsylvania, businessmen—and more importantly, the personal fortitude to create the system. Moreover, neither she nor her investors were forced to disentangle any aspect of their project from administrative or legislative red tape, a feat that would be quite near impossible today. The Geisinger Health Plan (GHP) was the first rural pilot HMO in Pennsylvania and is the largest rural HMO in the nation. Members receive care from more than 1,500 Geisinger staff and panel doctors who have affiliations with local hospitals and medical centers. GHP has the lowest administrative cost of any HMO in Pennsylvania.

The George F. Geisinger Memorial Hospital has evolved into the Geisinger regional health system, an array of separate not-for-profit corporate entities under the control of the Geisinger Foundation and serving more than two million people in Pennsylvania and southern New York. System components include the Geisinger Medical Center, a 548-bed tertiary care teaching hospital in Danville, Pennsylvania; Geisinger Wyoming Valley Medical Center (Wilkes-Barre, Pennsylvania), a 216-bed secondary care referral center; Marworth, a 77-bed addiction treatment center (Waverly, Pennsylvania); GHP, a 200,000-member HMO; and the Geisinger Clinic, a 500-member multispecialty group practice. The Geisinger Health System has received national recognition as a model for quality health service delivery and has been listed in *Best Hospitals in America*, and its physicians have been cited in *The Best Doctors in America*.

In spite of its tremendous expansion and diversification, GHS touted itself as striving to remain true to its original vision—that of meeting the health needs of individuals and communities throughout central Pennsylvania and beyond. Part of GHS's strategy is to create practice sites within 20 to 30 minutes' driving time, which would improve accessibility throughout the system. Doctors and management hopefully would collaborate to determine how resources could be most effectively distributed throughout the system and in such a way that it provides an optimal level of care to the community; herein supposedly lay the beauty of physician-led managed care as opposed to the traditional HMO approach.

While this approach has been invaluable to GHS, as a

not-for-profit jockeying for a position in a market dominated by investor-owned firms, it has been essential to reassess management structure and corporate tactics, particularly with respect to the increasing emphasis on vertical integration of services and managed care. In 1990, GHS executives identified strategies they felt would be imperative in navigating the health care environment of the future:

- GHS functions as one organization.

- Clinical programs and clinical process improvements determine the size and direction of the GHS.

- Managed care is GHS's primary business strategy.

- GHS seeks collaborative opportunities to increase access to cost-effective services.

This approach also focused on paying employees wages and benefits that were competitive in the marketplace. Merging with the HMC would permit GHS to pay competitively and cut costs. Thus, in July 1997, the merger was finalized.

## GHS EMPLOYEE COMPENSATION PACKAGES

When the merger occurred, two groups of employees were unionized at the HMC: nurses and technical service employees (i.e., electricians, etc.). Because the nurses' contract expired a few months before the merger was finalized, their representatives continued to negotiate a new contract. The Teamsters represent technical service personnel; the contract that HMC held with this group remained intact and will be honored by Penn State GHS until its expiration in 1999.

Annual sick and vacation time is accrued on an hourly basis per pay period throughout GHS. Employees were given several alternatives from which they might select life and health insurance, though they were understandably "encouraged" to choose GHP to accommodate their health care needs. Most GHS employees were required to contribute to the cost of their health care coverage.

# THE PENN STATE–GHS MERGER

Reminiscent of betrothals of dowry-laden females to noble young princes in a more patriarchal time, the conglomeration of the Penn State HMC and GHS was conceived and agreed to by a very small circle of upper-echelon decision makers at both organizations in a series of clandestine meetings. HMC and GHS had been jousting for the same central Pennsylvania market for years. Both were not-for-profit entities, both shared a common history, and both were facing a managed care environment that appeared intimidating at best, particularly for not-for-profit facilities. HMC and GHS had been restructuring to improve efficiency since early 1995, and—on paper, at least—the merger would enable the organizations to achieve their already planned cost reductions totaling $105 million over the first three years.

Throughout the Penn State system, employees had mixed feelings with respect to the announcement of the consolidation. Many employees in the Penn State community at large weren't very affected, though many were sad to see the HMC go. As for feelings in and around HMC, many employees initially underwent a period of denial, followed by resignation and, eventually, productive activity. There were painful moments during the transition in which people walked out of meetings, unwilling or unable to accept what appeared to be "things that Geisinger laid out that Penn State would never have agreed to." Eventually top management hoped, however, that Penn State GHS employees would grow accustomed to the transformed HMC and would continue to make positive contributions to the organization.

While salaries and wages did not immediately change as a result of the merger, they are now considered to be "market-driven"; Penn State GHS breadwinners no longer enjoy the same market-proof vacuum that their public and quasi-public counterparts do. Although their paychecks have not diminished, many employees found that their responsibilities have increased somewhat, as the environment at HMC may be characterized as "more of a business atmosphere" where management's priorities have changed.

With regard to benefits, those employees who participated in the SERS retirement plan as Penn State employees "had to convert" to a different plan; those who participated in

TIAA-CREF were able to continue. Annual leave time has been curtailed for many staff employees (i.e., the five service days to which they were entitled as compensation for the "University holidays"). One issue is whether Penn State GHS employees are given an alternative to GHP in selecting their health care provider. The answer is affirmative; nevertheless, management has let it be known that "it is to your advantage to participate in GHP."

Educational privileges stand as one of the benefits that are irreplaceable and will be sorely missed by former Penn State employees. The university was able to "grandfather in" many HMC staff members, providing them with a six-year window in which they may still obtain the 75-percent grant-in-aid tuition contribution from Penn State for themselves and their dependents. Nevertheless, many people went to work for Penn State precisely because they (or their families) would be eligible both for educational privileges at a high-caliber university and to be a part of the Nittany Lion family pride. Now they must cope with the fact that they are no longer Nittany Lions.

## DISCUSSION

1.  If you had been planning the Penn State–Geisinger merger, what approach and strategy would you have taken in preparing Penn State employees for the transition?

2.  What advice would you give Abner Hamm and his coworkers regarding how to deal with the merger? Should they investigate organizing a bargaining unit and seek union recognition?

3.  What are the advantages and disadvantages to former Penn State employees of the new Penn State GHS compensation package?

# 7

## MERIT SYSTEM STANDARDS

# Hiring the Unqualified

*Congress of the United States*
*House of Representatives*
*Washington, DC 20515-0502*
*Congressman Wally Herger's Comments*
*Regarding USDA Civil Rights Programs*
*Woodland, California*
*January 17, 1997*

I appreciate Secretary Glickman's leadership in providing this forum for both federal employees and the interested public to discuss United States Department of Agriculture [USDA] civil rights programs. I am a strong supporter of the Civil Rights Act of 1964.

The laudable goal of that landmark piece of legislation was the abolition of discrimination. Regrettably, the USDA civil rights programs fall far short of that lofty goal. Indeed, current USDA civil rights programs show an obsession with matters of race and gender, and an unfair and counterproductive commitment to quotas in both hiring and promotion opportunities.

I will submit for the record today United States Forest Service job announcements that specify that—and I am now quoting from these job postings—"Only Unqualified Appli-

cants May Apply," "Only Applicants Who Do Not Meet X-118
Standards Will Be Considered," and "Only Applicants Who
Do Not Meet the OPM Qualifications Requirements Will Be
Considered Under This Announcement."

Mr. Secretary, I submit to you that it is not a civil right
to land a job for which one is unqualified. If we, as a nation,
are to ever move beyond conflicts over race and gender, we
must become color-blind. We must let excellence be our
standard, because excellence can come and does come in a
variety of colors. We must return to the original vision of Dr.
Martin Luther King, Jr., who hoped for a day in which all of
us are judged by the content of our character, and not the
color of our skin.

The affirmative action programs of the USDA are nothing more than quota programs. As such, they are divisive
and morally indefensible. They guarantee workplace hostil-
ity, and set race relations backward, not forward. They stig-
matize the very people who are supposed to benefit from the
program. What message is sent to the employee who applies
for a position requiring that he or she demonstrate that he
or she has not yet met minimal standards associated with
the position? This is ludicrous, and it must end.

We cannot remedy past discrimination by engaging in
more discrimination. The best solution for past discrimination is no more discrimination at all.

I have heard from hundreds of Forest Service employees who have deluged my office with job announcements
that contain bizarre preconditions that effectively preclude
them from the advertised position.

I will provide to you today a job announcement that contains the requirement that the successful applicant must show
a (quote) "demonstrated commitment to civil rights or contribution to a diverse workforce." Forest Service employees have
complained that this appears to be "code language" designed
to exclude many otherwise qualified nonminority males.

By USDA definition, nonminority males do not contribute to a diverse workforce. And how is the job applicant
expected to "demonstrate" his commitment to the Forest
Service civil rights program? This appears to require the
passing of an ideological litmus test as a requirement for
employment or promotion. This has an Orwellian overtone,
and is flatly wrong.

Many of my constituents who are Forest Service employees do not support the USDA civil rights programs, and are involved in a lawsuit to protest this kind of quota hiring. These employees surely do not demonstrate a commitment to the program over which they are suing and thus they are, by definition, unable to meet the evaluation criteria for this advertised position.

Not only is quota hiring unfair and divisive, it can also be dangerous. I am today submitting a "white paper" produced by the Plumas National Forest, in which the following statements appeared:

"In a growing number of instances, we are not filling positions when there are no women applicants. In the past three months we have readvertised, left vacant, or filled with unqualified temporaries 11 permanent fire positions because we could not find female applicants. If the position is in fire prevention or forest fuels management, the job simply doesn't get done and we face the consequences of additional person-caused fires and untreated hazardous forest fuels."

The Plumas attempted to fill five positions from the roster, but could reach only two women. "Both women declined our offers. No offers were made to men. All fire positions are presently vacant or filled with unqualified temporary employees."

I find the preceding statements both shocking and appalling. Regrettably, it was not an isolated incident. Both public safety and our natural resources can clearly be compromised by this wrong-headed policy.

Quota hiring is also expensive. The quota hiring system has led to an explosion of Equal Employment Opportunity Commission [EEOC] complaints within the Forest Service. Forest Service employees have informed me that the costs of these EEOC complaints, including sizable financial awards, are often "charged" to the timber or fire budget of the affected forest. Thus, we see less money committed to the resources on the ground as available funding is consumed by contentious legal squabbles. This situation is a disservice to both the taxpayers and our federal employees.

On several occasions, my inquiries to the Forest Service regarding this matter have been met with the response that, while these problems may have existed many years ago, they have now been corrected. Regrettably, there are recent job postings that clearly indicate that quotas are, in fact, the status quo within USDA. I have attached samples of these documents for your review.

Mr. Secretary, I urge you to scrap the current fatally flawed quota system and install in its place a merit- and skill-based approach to both hiring and promotions.

Because the Forest Service civil rights program has been particularly harmful, I have introduced legislation—the "Forest Service Employment Opportunity Act of 1997"—to assist the Forest Service in moving beyond the failed status quo. I encourage the administration to support this legislative remedy.

Working together, we can put past problems behind us by fashioning hiring and promotion policies that are fair to everyone. The current programs have clearly failed to achieve the desired outcomes of nondiscrimination and fairness. USDA can and should do better. Thank you.

## DISCUSSION

1.    Discuss your reasons for either continuing or discontinuing the Forest Service's practice of filling certain designated positions by unqualified applicants.

2.    What is the implied correlation between an increase in EEOC complaints and the filling of positions with unqualified applicants?

3.    What options are available for achieving the Forest Service's goal of increased diversity without compromising the merit system?

# 8

## PERSONNEL RECORDS MANAGEMENT

# Dissing the Border Patrol

*It's no secret that the highly paid and prestigious agency of the FBI and the Assistant U.S. Attorneys have little respect for the Border Patrol, whom they view as lower class grunts akin to pigs. Neither do Border Patrol officers feel very kindly toward the suit-and-tie guys who look down on the people in the field. Oftentimes, officers believe the FBI and U.S. Attorneys seem to be out to trap Border Patrol officers rather than trying to stem the rising tide of "illegals" that are pouring into this country.*

Sam Allen thought that when he joined the U.S. Border Patrol (BP) in November of 1984 it would be a lot different than it turned out to be in reality. Allen had imagined days filled with intrigue and high adventure spent chasing down illegal aliens from Mexico and Central America who tried to sneak into the United States illegally near the Sonora-Arizona border. However, instead of excitement, Allen underwent a daily round of boring, thankless work that only occasionally provided any interesting relief. Much of his time was either spent on patrol in the hot, high Sonoran desert or manning checkpoints along interstates checking cars for illegal aliens. Allen particularly hated the checkpoints because so many citizens were offended when they believed their privacy was being invaded by the intrusive questioning of BP officers. Despite these disappointments, Allen fully intended to continue his work and took pride in doing a difficult job in spite of adverse circumstances. What Allen could not have foreseen was a series of events that resulted in a permanent blot on his personnel record by the U.S. Attorney, which ruined Allen's reputation and career. It all started with an unfortunate discharge of weapons on a cool desert night.

## THE 1992 SHOOTING INCIDENTS

Late during the evening of March 18, 1992, several BP officers, including Sam Allen and Jim Ellsworth, were performing line-watch duties with the assistance of National Guardsmen, who spotted a group of illegal aliens—possibly armed—entering the United States. Allen and Ellsworth followed up on this information and proceeded along a road called "A Road." At one point, they became separated and Allen became aware that he was walking alone in the dark terrain. About 30 minutes later, Allen heard gunshots from the direction in which had last seen Ellsworth. Allen was so startled by the shots that he accidentally discharged his drawn revolver, firing two rounds into the ground. Allen continued walking along the trail until he bumped into a group of illegal aliens and promptly arrested them. However, Officer Allen failed to report that night or thereafter his weapon discharge or that he heard shots because he "was too embarrassed."

Nonetheless, the U.S. Border Patrol's *Administrative Manual* (Par. 9) states:

> In each incident involving discharge of a firearm, regardless of the circumstances, a radio or telephonic report shall be made immediately. A verbal report shall be made to the front-line supervisor as soon as time and circumstance permit, but not later than the end of the tour of duty in which the incident occurred. Within sixteen hours of each incident the participating Service employee shall furnish a written report, through the supervisory channels, to the District Director or the Chief Patrol Agent having jurisdiction over the place where the incident occurred.

Officer Allen was aware of the requirement to report both the gunshots he heard and the discharge of his own weapon.

On June 12, 1992, Officer Ellsworth was involved in a tragic incident during which he shot and killed Armas Villa, an illegal alien who was attempting to run around a roadblock near Bisbee, Arizona. The shooting received widespread media attention in Arizona and throughout the United States. Officer Allen was on vacation when the shooting occurred but subsequently was drawn into the investigation because investigators had heard of previous incidents of mysterious gunshots.

In September of 1992, the Office of the Inspector General at the Immigration and Naturalization Service (INS) launched an investigation of the shooting incident, and Officer Allen was also subpoenaed to testify. Allen was first interviewed by Officer Ray Muldoon on September 15, 1992, wherein he was questioned primarily about the March 18 incident. In his signed affidavit, Allen stated, "I also deny saying that I recall firing my weapon at all (and I say this only to account for your statement that two weapons fired) it would have been as a reaction to being surprised by the first string of gunfire. That may have happened, but the weapon certainly would have been pointed at the ground." A week later, Officer Allen was called back; at that time he told Officer Muldoon that he had had time to think it over, and there was no doubt in his mind that, in fact, he did fire his weapon into the ground. Allen also told Muldoon that he realized that he could be subject to disciplinary action, and he signed a revised affidavit.

## THE TRIAL AND AFTERMATH

In December of 1992, Officer Ellsworth was brought to trial for the murder of Armas Villa in the U.S. District Court for Arizona. Officer Allen was called as witness for the prosecution, and during direct examination and cross-examination he repeated the statements contained in his original and revised affidavits. Officer Ellsworth was acquitted, but the federal prosecution decided to gain Ellsworth's conviction by charging him with a violation of Villa's civil rights. Officer Allen voluntarily appeared at a pretrial conference where he was subjected to accusatory questioning regarding unexplained gunshots on previous occasions by three Assistant

U.S. Attorneys. Later, Allen appeared at a federal grand jury. On each occasion, Allen told about what had happened during the March 18 incident. Despite the best efforts of the federal prosecution, Officer Ellsworth was acquitted by the jury a second time in February of 1994.

Twelve days after the acquittal of Ellsworth and approximately 11 months following Officer Allen's last appearance before a grand jury, U.S. District Attorney Janet Napoli sent a letter, dated February 15, 1994, to Curt Dowling, then chief patrol officer in the Tucson sector, which included the following paragraph:

> I unfortunately must inform you that my office has concluded that we will no longer work with or sponsor two of your agents from the Nogales, Arizona, office. We believe these men have testified either untruthfully or misleadingly about facts of which they had personal knowledge. Their testimony occurred before either the federal jury or the U.S. District Court and concerned allegations that former Border Patrol Officer Ellsworth assaulted several individuals at the border. They also made inaccurate or untruthful statements to agents with the Department of Justice's Office of Inspector General concerning the Ellsworth allegations. In addition, Officers Ellsworth and Allen failed to cooperate in a manner commensurate with their responsibilities as law enforcement officials.

The U.S. Attorney and her staff had found their scapegoats for the loss of two federal trials.

On September 26, 1994, almost nine months later, Deputy Border Patrol Chief Ray Coffey cited two incidents as reasons for his decision to propose the dismissal of Officer Allen: (1) his failure to report the discharge of his weapon and the shots Allen heard from another direction on March 18, (2) Allen's inability to perform the full range of the duties of his position due to the limitations created by U.S. Attorney Napoli's letter. Coffey referenced two job factors from the position description for border patrol officer as the basis of his decision:

> *Factor 5.* The purpose of the work assignment is to enforce the Immigration and Nationality Act and related statutes.

The Agent's competence and conduct in completing assignments and subsequent court testimony as required determines to a large extent whether it will be possible to gain convictions of those who have been apprehended.

*Factor 6.* It is the duty of patrol agents not only to bring to justice violations of criminal laws within the jurisdiction of the Service, but to assist in the successful prosecution of such offenders.

----

Coffey reasoned that because the U.S. Attorney's office no longer had confidence in Officer Allen or could allow him to testify under oath, Allen was not able to perform all of his job duties. Coffey admitted that Napoli's letter was a paramount consideration in his mind, "Had it not been for the Napoli letter, I would have proposed a lesser discipline than removal. Just the plain fact that someone discharged his weapon and failed to report it would not lead to removal."

Coffey's recommendation was forwarded to Curt Dowling, chief patrol officer, who sustained both charges in his decision letter of September 7, 1995. Officer Allen was separated from the INS on September 15, 1995.

## UNSUBSTANTIATED ALLEGATIONS

Napoli's letter was vague and ambiguous concerning the reasons for her decision; also, the charges are extremely serious. Officer Allen and his attorney made repeated attempts to seek clarification and specific evidence for Napoli's decision, but none was forthcoming. Napoli steadfastly refused to clarify her reasons. She simply announced that she would not allow Officer Allen and two other officers to testify in BP cases, even though testifying was a critical element of an agent's job.

"How can they do this to me?" Allen asked his attorney. The collective bargaining agreement clearly prohibits putting unsubstantiated allegations in an employee personnel file:

*Article 32. Section K.* No record of complaint, determined to be unfounded, shall be placed in the employee's official personnel folder. Such complaint may, in the interest of

> the employee and the Service, be maintained in a subject
> file but will not under any circumstance be considered as
> a factor in connection with any disciplinary action, pro-
> motion, or personnel action.

———————

Allen's attorney agreed, "You're absolutely right, only factual matters may be placed in an employee's personnel file. Matters of opinion, such as a performance evaluation, may also be entered but they are not supposed to be used publicly to hurt someone's career or reputation."

At the predisciplinary predetermination hearing, Curt Dowling admitted that he understood an employee is entitled to know the charges against him and the reasons why a job might be taken away. Dowling confessed that he and Coffey did not, as a basis for discharge, sustain any allegation that Allen testified falsely in connection with the Villa trial. Napoli's charges were unfounded, "but if she sends me a letter saying she won't use these witnesses, they can't do their jobs, regardless of her reasons, the letter will remain in his file forever."

## DISCUSSION

1.  Where should the letter from U.S. Attorney Napoli be kept? Should it be placed in a file apart from the official employee folder?

2.  What guidelines and criteria would you establish for deciding which documents are placed in an employee's personnel file? At what point and how should employee files with derogatory information be expunged?

3.  The Border Patrol has clearly been placed between the proverbial rock and a hard place by Napoli's letter. How would you recommend that Coffey and Dowling handle the matter?

# II

# EMPLOYMENT RELATIONS

# 9

## COLLECTIVE BARGAINING
## (PROBLEM SOLVING)

# Handling the Hanford Patrol

*Employees at the Hanford Test Site of the U.S. Department of Energy were very much aware that they were viewed by Washington, D.C., headquarters as a bunch of country bumpkins out in eastern Washington State. They had heard many times the derogatory comments by Beltway inhabitants, for example, referring to the "tri-cities" in Washington State as "trog cities."*

The security guards who work at the Hanford facility were growing increasingly impatient with Westinghouse management. Most of the guards had been longtime employees of the EG&G Corporation, which had been the original contractor with the U.S. Department of Energy (DOE) to manage the Hanford Test Site in eastern Washington State. However, two years ago DOE awarded the management contract to the Westinghouse Corporation, which agreed to continue employment of all guards in the Hanford Patrol.

It soon became apparent that Westinghouse managers were socialized to a much more business-oriented organizational culture than the "we are family" orientation practiced by EG&G. Relations between the International Guards Union (IGU) and the Westinghouse management team began deteriorating immediately. The atmosphere was further polarized when management discharged two guards, one a union steward, for allegedly drinking beer in the parking lot, only to have both decisions reversed in separate arbitration decisions that reinstated both employees. Morale among the guards had reached its lowest ebb since the facility's creation.

Tensions reached the breaking point in January when DOE announced revised Active Force Physical Activity Requirements (AFPAR) for security guards employed by its subcontractors, including guards in the Hanford Patrol. Spurred by rising fears in DOE headquarters of possible terrorist activities directed against DOE facilities, AFPAR was hailed as a means of molding contractor security forces into responsive "lean and mean machines." All DOE subcontractors were given one year to weed out any security guards who could not meet AFPAR standards.

The revised AFPAR standards required that guards be able to run three miles in under 30 minutes and, upon the run's completion, to immediately fire a semiautomatic .45 six times, hitting a target in vital areas with at least four shots. Formerly, guards were mandated only to run a 12-minute mile each September and maintain shooting certification at the firing range. To complicate matters, Hanford Patrol members had a much older average age (37.5 years) than other DOE subcontractors nationwide. The average employment tenure with the Hanford Patrol was 15 years. Other law enforcement agencies in the area generally did not give credit for work experience as security guards.

AFPAR standards were not a negotiable subject for collective bargaining because of federal guidelines, and Westinghouse managers initially refused even to discuss the matter with the IGU but later agreed to hold informal "discussions." It is now March, and teams from both sides are ready to explore their respective positions, even though there is very little optimism on either side.

## HANFORD PATROL TEAMS

Assume that your negotiating team is composed of five members, which include a representative from the IGU, the two stewards who were reinstated, and two members elected by the rank-and-file because of their reputations for militancy. The team is very concerned about the potential loss of employment for a large number of guards who would not currently be able to meet the new AFPAR standards. There is no way the team members can allow guards to be laid off without a fight, even if it means a strike (although a strike would generally not be illegal for private contractor employees, the courts might take a dim view of a walkout over an issue not subject to collective bargaining). Several team members suspect that AFPAR standards are a ruse to get rid of more costly and older guards, largely white males, and to replace them with younger, lower-paid employees, many of whom would be women and minorities.

## WESTINGHOUSE MANAGEMENT TEAM

Assume that this negotiating team is also composed of five members, which include the following individuals, all of whom were Westinghouse employees prior to coming to Hanford: the general manager, the human resources director, the chief financial officer, the legal counsel, and the commander of the Hanford Patrol. You are all well aware that Westinghouse succeeded, in large part, in taking the Hanford contract away from EG&G because of promises made to DOE to improve productivity while curtailing rising costs. Your team has been warned by corporate headquarters that it is not about to go back to DOE in an effort to have the AFPAR standards modified. The company is determined to prove its managerial capability to DOE in hopes of gaining future contracts at Rocky Flats and Savannah River. However, the prospect of a work stoppage is also disturbing and would not win points for Westinghouse with DOE.

## DISCUSSION

1.  The Hanford Patrol scenario occurs in an environment in which parties consider their respective negotiation styles as adversaries. During negotiation simulation, each team member should analyze and reflect in a jour-

nal the negotiating styles and tactics within the team and horizontally between the teams.

2.   At the conclusion of a "problem-solving" negotiation simulation, the parties are to compare styles and tactics as well as identify the actual needs of both sides.

3.   Did both teams successfully escape the temptation to negotiate from positions rather than as problem solvers?

# 10

## COLLECTIVE BARGAINING
## (POSITIONAL)

# Taking the
# Firefighters' Heat

*Great negotiators are not "naturals" who simply possess
some hidden talent unknown to others. Effective negotiation requires skill building that can be perfected only
through knowledge and repetitive practice, on a regular
basis, in each negotiating situation. Positional bargaining is a strategy that is based on moving from position to
position, without revealing one's true agenda, until compromise is reached. Unlike problem-solving negotiation,
which has been called "getting to yes," positional bargaining is more like "getting to OK."*

The city of Concord, New Hampshire, has a population of
50,000 inhabitants, and its city hall is currently preparing for
negotiations with the International Association of Fire Fighters
(IAFF) local #37, which represents the 120 full-time firefighters
and paramedics who are deployed among seven station houses.
Both parties are approaching the upcoming negotiations with
some trepidation because labor-management relations under
the present collective bargaining agreement have been anything but harmonious.

## THE CITY'S POSITION

The city's negotiating team consists of three members: the personnel director, budget director, and the chief of the fire department. The first two are classified employees, while the chief is a political appointee and longtime friend of the mayor.

Currently, Concord Fire Department (CFD) employees in the bargaining unit earn an average of $30,000 per year in wages, plus a generous benefit package calculated as worth another $20,000 per employee. Thus, the compensation package for CFD employees totals some $6 million for represented employees, approximately $700,000 for six managers (the chief and five assistant chiefs), and almost $250,000 for two secretaries and five dispatchers.

Traditionally, overtime costs have run approximately $7.2 million annually. Management has been advised by an outside consultant to consider flexing work schedules so that it can avoid paying excessive overtime, but this proposal would certainly be strongly opposed by the union. Negotiations also are expected to center on issues of pay, health insurance, and annual leave time, with management needing to hold down costs as much as possible.

Management's position is exacerbated by the fact that neighboring Manchester, a city of approximately 100,000 citizens, pays its firefighters and paramedics an average of $2,000 per year more than does Concord, provides comparable benefits, and allows a week more annual leave (three to five weeks, depending on seniority, in contrast to the two to four weeks given by CFD). Increased annual leave would mean hiring more employees, and the mayor is adamantly opposed to new hires. The negotiating team believes that the union will want a package similar to the Manchester Fire Department (MFD), but the mayor has ordered the management team to hold the line on labor costs.

Budget projections for next year are pessimistic, and layoffs will be needed if labor costs go up. The city's negotiating team has been instructed that it may spend no more than $7.5 million per year for the next two years, and it may negotiate only a two-year contract. The rising cost of health care means that positions must be eliminated or compensation decreased if the city is to remain within budget projections.

The management team has been authorized to threaten the union, if necessary, with layoffs and even with closure of one of the fire stations. As far as health care is concerned, the mayor is not opposed to increasing copayments (currently employees pay $5 per prescription and $5 per office visit), employee contribution to health care premiums (currently workers pay nothing, and all family members are included), or a preferred provider program (currently employees have a choice of physicians and hospitals).

The current Collective Bargaining Agreement provides a 3-percent per year raise in wages, two-weeks' annual leave for employees with one to five years in service, three weeks for those employees with six to ten years, and four weeks for employees with more than ten years in service. The union has indicated that it will seek a 6-percent wage increase for the first year of the upcoming contract, and 4 percent for each year thereafter included in the agreement. The union would like a long-term contract of three or four years and it would also like to hold steady on health care benefits as well as more annual leave.

## THE UNION'S POSITION

The union's negotiating team consists of three negotiators: a professional negotiator from the IAFF, the local's president, and the secretary-treasurer of local #37. There is some smoldering resentment among rank-and-file members, who feel that they put their lives on the line for an average of $30,000 in wages while the five assistant chiefs each have hefty salaries averaging $80,000, and the chief makes in excess of $100,000 annually. Most of the assistant chiefs and the chief were formerly active in the union before crossing over to the management side.

As indicated, current negotiations are centered on pay, health insurance, and annual leave, but the most irritating fact is that Concord firefighters and paramedics are treated so much worse than Manchester employees with similar jobs. Concord employees believe that they are just as good as their Manchester counterparts and deserve comparable pay and benefits. A 6-percent raise during the first year of the next contract would close the gap between CFD and MFD, and 4 percent for each year thereafter would enable Concord workers to hold steady in comparison with Manchester. The unit membership has insisted that the negotiating team hold steady on health care benefits and they would like annual leave comparable to MFD.

The union's negotiation team has heard the city's usual lament regarding fiscal stress and the need for restraint. It has also been subjected to the usual threats of layoffs but the union feels that all of these excuses mask an indifference to the dedication and professionalism of CFD's employees. Even though Manchester is a larger city than Concord, it has a lower median income level. The union team is convinced that its first task will be to convince the city to take the issue of parity with Manchester seriously by negotiating in good faith. Concord firefighters have authorized a strike in an unofficial vote, even though it is illegal under state law, if parity with Manchester is not achieved through collective bargaining.

## DISCUSSION

1.  If you were the team leader for the labor team, what instructions for positional bargaining would you give to your team?

2.  You are the team leader for the management team. What instructions for positional bargaining would you give to your team?

3.  To what extent was it possible to negotiate from a positional approach without becoming too adversarial?

# 11

## LABOR-MANAGEMENT RELATIONS

# Holiday Time for Prison Guards

*Arbitrators are frequently called in when an impasse is reached between a union and management regarding the meaning of a clause within the Collective Bargaining Agreement (CBA). The arbitrator is charged with resolving the impasse by applying accepted standards or criteria for interpreting unclear and ambiguous language. One criterion is whether past workplace practices constitute a de facto understanding; another criterion is the intent of the negotiators of the CBA when they originally wrote the clause. At times, these two criteria are seemingly contradictory.*

## BACKGROUND

Gregory George is a sergeant with the Western New Mexico Correctional Facility (WNMCF) in Grants, New Mexico. He is a classified employee and a member of a bargaining unit, local #3422 of the American Federation of State, County, and Municipal Employees (AFSCME). Sgt. George had accrued 24 hours (three days) of holiday compensatory time by May 1993 and was informed by his supervisor, Lt. Ethan Carlson, that this time would need to be taken prior to June 18, the last available date prior to the end of the fiscal year. Lt. Carlson stated that he was simply complying with a directive from the WNMCF warden and departmental authorities to require all hourly employees to take compensatory time earned by working holidays prior to the beginning of the next fiscal year. It was also departmental practice to schedule compensatory time, if at all possible, rather than paying for hours accrued.

Lt. Carlson apprised Sgt. George that he had a choice of several dates as holiday compensatory time off but it would not be permissible to choose days in the next fiscal year. Sgt. George declined to select days in May or June and reiterated his desire to use holiday compensatory time in conjunction with the Independence Day weekend in July, which fit into long-standing plans to attend a feast day with his family at nearby Zuni Pueblo Reservation. Lt. Carlson refused Sgt. George's request and scheduled him for June 3, 4, and 5, 1994; these days were in conjunction with George's regular days off and prior to the end of the fiscal year. Sgt. George was extremely upset and went to see his union steward, who consulted the CBA. According to Article XII.B. of the "Collective Bargaining Agreement" between New Mexico Department of Corrections and AFSCME Local #3422 (January 29, 1993–January 29, 1995), the following conditions for using compensatory time are in effect:

> Employees required to work on the day a holiday is observed shall be compensated at a rate as authorized by the rules of the State Personnel Board. Such compensation may be in cash or compensatory time. To the extent that such payment is to be made in the form of compensatory time, the following conditions shall prevail:
>
> 1. The date to be taken as compensatory time off shall be scheduled by agreement between the supervisor and the employee.
>
> 2. If for any reason the scheduled date cannot be honored, the supervisor and the employee shall select another day for the compensatory time off to be taken as soon thereafter as practicable.

The union steward reviewed the CBA clause and exclaimed, "It's just as I thought—this language is clear and unambiguous regarding holiday compensatory time; it must be scheduled on a mutually agreed date by the employee and supervisor. The department cannot allege extenuating circumstances just because of the fiscal year's end. Its requirement that holiday compensatory time be taken prior to the end of the fiscal year violates Article XII.B."

Following review by the local's grievance review committee, Sgt. George and the union decided to pursue arbitration and ask the arbitrator to award the following as a remedy: Pay for holiday compensatory time that George was required to take and to compel the department to cease its practice of requiring employees to use accrued holiday compensatory time prior to the fiscal year's completion.

When presented with Sgt. George's grievance, the department contended that it did not violate its CBA with the union based on the following reasons:

1.  Article III of the CBA, "Management Rights and State Personnel Board Rules," allows the department to schedule days off.

2.  Article XII.B. is not an absolute right and must be understood in harmony with the entire CBA.

3.  The department has a long-standing practice of scheduling holiday compensatory time to meet management's scheduling needs.

4.  Purposes of "sound fiscal management" require that holiday compensatory time not be carried over into another fiscal year.

5   Sgt. George's supervisor made a reasonable effort to accommodate him by providing a block of time during which he could select days for holiday compensatory time.

After much discussion and negotiation, the union and management were unable to resolve the issue by agreeing on a common understanding of what the CBA intended as guidelines on this issue.

However, both parties stipulated the issue to be arbitrated as follows:

Did the Department violate Article XII.B. of the CBA by requiring the Grievant to request his holiday compensatory time be scheduled off before the end of the fiscal year; and when Grievant failed or refused to make such a request, by unilaterally scheduling the Grievant off for certain days before the end of the fiscal year on holiday compensatory time?

The two sides were now ready to present their impasse to the arbitrator.

## INTERPRETING THE CBA ON COMPENSATORY TIME

The arbitrator heard evidence and testimony from the union and management at the arbitration hearing, most of which focused on two considerations: (1) what the negotiators had meant to articulate when they agreed to the current CBA, and (2) past workplace practices when scheduling compensatory time.

## WHAT THE NEGOTIATORS MEANT TO SAY

The CBA between the Department of Corrections and AFSCME local #3422 went into effect on January 29, 1993, and was due to expire on January 29, 1995. Negotiations between the department and union commenced on or about September 18, 1991, and continued for approximately 13 months, during which a number of proposals and counterproposals regarding holiday pay were considered by the parties. Previous CBAs between the parties had included the following language in Article XII.B. concerning "Holidays":

Employees required to work on the day a holiday is observed shall be compensated at a rate as authorized by rules of the State Personnel Board. Such compensation nay be in cash or compensatory time.

_____

Under this language, supervisors simply scheduled holiday compensatory time, often without consulting employees. Consequently, AFSCME negotiators during the fall of 1991 proposed the following language for contract inclusion:

Employees who are required to work on a day that is observed as a holiday shall be compensated at the rate of two-and-one-half times the hourly rate of pay or granted compensatory time at the rate of two-and one-half times the regular rate of pay. The choice of compensatory time or wages shall be made by the employee. All such hours worked shall be counted for the purpose of computing overtime. An employee need not have forty (40) hours of work in order to qualify for this holiday pay rate.

Departmental negotiators rejected the concept that an employee could choose either compensatory time or wages for time worked on holidays. Instead, the department team proposed the following article on December 12, 1991, which was incorporated into the CBA:

### Holidays

A. Legal public holidays shall be observed as prescribed by statute and regulations of the State Personnel Board.

B. Employees required to work on the day a holiday is observed shall be compensated at a rate as authorized by the rules of the State Personnel Board. Such compensation may be in cash or compensatory time. To the extent that such payment is to be made in the form of compensatory time, the following conditions shall prevail:

1. The date to be taken as compensatory time off shall be scheduled by agreement between the supervisor and the employee.

2. If for any reason, the scheduled date cannot be honored, the supervisor and the employee shall select another date for the compensatory time off to be taken as soon thereafter as practicable.

In addition to the CBA, members of the bargaining unit were also governed by rules and regulations passed by the State Personnel Board. State Personnel Board Rule 6.12, adopted January 2, 1993, was adopted prior to the current CBA and implements the following provisions:

## Holiday Pay

A. Employees required to work on the day a holiday is observed shall be compensated at two-and-one-half times the usual hourly rate of pay for all hours actually worked on the holiday.

B. Employees not required to work on the day a holiday is observed shall be compensated at their hourly rate of pay for the number of hours they would have worked.

C. Part-time employees whose normal work schedule does not include the day a holiday is observed shall not be compensated for the holiday.

Within a month following ratification of the current CBA, the State Personnel Board revised Rule 6.12, "Holiday Pay," as follows:

## Holiday Pay

A. When a holiday falls on an employee's regularly scheduled workday and the employee is not required to work, the employee shall be compensated in cash payment at their usual hourly rate of pay for the number of hours he or she would have normally worked.

B. Employees required to work on the day a holiday is observed shall be compensated at two-and-one-half times the usual hourly rate of pay for all hours worked on the holiday. Such compensation shall be in the form of straight-time cash payment for all hours actually worked and additional premium compensation, at the agency's discretion, of either compensatory time off or cash payment at one-and-one-half times the usual hourly rate of pay for all hours actually worked. It is strongly suggested that employee requests for compensatory time off be honored by agencies on a priority basis.

C. Part-time employees whose normal work schedule
does not include the day a holiday is observed shall
not be compensated for the holiday.

Thus, the CBA and State Personnel Board Rules included
employee preferences as a factor to be considered when
scheduling holiday compensatory time.

## THE PRECEDENCE OF DEPARTMENTAL PAST PRACTICES

Despite giving employee preference a role in deciding when
holiday compensatory time would be scheduled, the department and union agreed in Article III.6 of the CBA that "Management retains the right to determine scheduling and all
other actions necessary to carry out Department functions."
It was a long-standing past practice of the Department of
Corrections to schedule as much holiday compensatory leave
as possible prior to the fiscal year's conclusion, although it
was apparently never totally able to reach this goal and
would either carry over a small amount of "comp time" or pay
leave to a few employees.

The department's aforementioned policy was determined at the cabinet secretary's level and implemented by
the Administrative Services Division as well as the respective
wardens. No evidence was produced at the arbitration hearing to indicate that the policy of mandatory scheduling of holiday compensatory time before conclusion of the fiscal year
emanated from other state authorities—Department of
Finance and Administration, General Services Department,
State Auditor—or by state statute.

## THE ARBITRATOR'S AWARD

Following review of the testimony, evidence, and arguments
presented during the arbitration hearing, the arbitrator
made the following points in his award:

• The language contained in Article XII.B. of the controlling CBA is clear and unambiguous: The dates to be taken as compensatory time off shall be scheduled by agreement between the supervisor and the employee.

• If, for any reason, the scheduled date cannot be honored, the supervisor and the employee shall select another date for the compensatory time off to be taken "as soon thereafter as practicable."

• State Personnel Board Rule 6.12 also is clear in its intent: "It is strongly suggested that employee requests for compensatory time off be honored by agencies on a priority basis." Arbitrators, like the courts, use a commonly accepted set of rules to interpret ambiguous or unclear contract language. These standards apply to evidence from outside the CBA and evidence contained within the CBA itself.

• However, the "parol evidence" rule holds that external evidence cannot be admitted for the purpose of changing or contradicting clearly written language. In other words, the parties are presumed to have meant what they wrote, and arbitration must enforce the terms as written. If language is unclear (its meaning undecipherable or ambiguous), then external criteria, that is, past practice, bargaining history, prior settlements, financial constraints, and the like, may be used to interpret language (along with internal evidence).

• Both parties were represented by experienced negotiating teams who are presumed to literally intend what the controlling language in Article XII.B. says, "The date to be taken as compensatory time shall be scheduled by agreement between the supervisor and the employee." This language supersedes past practices, which included supervisors dictating when leave would be scheduled and requiring leave to be used prior to the conclusion of the fiscal year.

• Finally, even though clear and unambiguous language was stated in the CBA article, parties to an agreement may amend or add to it by a subsequent agreement or memorandum of understanding. Although the CBA is the chief instrument that guides the parties in their relationships, there frequently arises an occasion when it is necessary to clarify the CBA in some manner. This is what a side agreement does. They are very commonly used because they are found to be useful. But until and unless a Memorandum of Understanding is negotiated regarding Article XII.B., clear and unambiguous language is controlling.

The arbitrator ordered that the provisions of Article XII.B. of the CBA be strictly enforced, whereby covered employees must agree to dates selected for holiday compensatory time. The arbitrator did not order the department to reimburse Sgt. George for three days of holiday compensatory time, because this remedy was not contained within the issue as stipulated by the union and management.

## DISCUSSION

1.  To what extent do you agree or disagree with the arbitrator's decision? What modifications, if any, would you have made in the arbitrator's decision?

2.  Is the language in the CBA sufficiently clear and unambiguous? How might it be modified by a Memorandum of Understanding?

3.  Assess from management and labor perspectives how you would attempt to modify the current CBA when planning for negotiations for the next one?

# 12

## AFFIRMATIVE ACTION

# An African American Woman Among the Good Ol' Boys in Indiana

*Whenever I hear terms describing college mascots, such as "Aggies," "Hoakies," and "Hoosiers," I envision "good ol' boys" of the white, redneck variety. I certainly can't envision African Americans ever referring to themselves by such names.*

President William Clinton
The White House
1600 Pennsylvania Ave. NW
Washington, DC 20500

Dear Mr. President:

I applaud you for taking the initiative in attempting to improve race relations in this country. Believe me, it is sorely needed.

Having just gone through horrendous experiences with the U.S. Forest Service [USFS], I am of the opinion that the first place that needs investigation are the federal agencies—specifically, the U.S. Forest Service. I believe this agency is a bastion of institutional racism. Are you aware, Mr. President, that there were thousands of complaints filed against this agency for harassment and racial discrimination within the last few years? Doesn't that tell you something is wrong?

As a 52-year-old African American employee of USFS, I was systematically forced to resign. I had to make a choice if I wanted to retain a modicum of my health and my sanity. I had to give up the benefits that I had accumulated through eight years of very hard work. Now, I *must* try to start all over because of harassment and discrimination by a male supervisor who did not like the color of my skin and who resented my abilities.

Prior to becoming employed by the federal government, I worked in private industry. I was a graduate assistant in a department of public administration during my college years; I have never received a poor evaluation nor was I ever dismissed from any position.

Through the years I had heard from federal employees about the "good ol' boys network" and how people's lives were ruined by it. Therefore, in 1986 when I was approached about becoming a federal employee, I gave the invitation a good deal of thought before giving my answer. I was also told there was a desperate need for accountants. Emphasis was made on the fact that not only were my employment credentials impeccable, but the USFS would benefit in their diversity program because I am a black female with a permanent handicap. After two years I finally decided to apply for a position and received a direct hire from the Office of Personnel Management (OPM); I got the job on the spot.

At the time I was hired I was the only black in my section and one of only three in the entire building. Shortly after entering the USFS, I received a GS-9 rating and performed well, despite suffering a brain aneurysm that caused me to be unable to work for almost a year. Upon my return, I was presented with an opportunity to upgrade to a GS-11 status by transferring to the Hoosier National Forest in Bedford, Indiana, for a position as a budget and accounting officer.

My only preconceptions of Indiana were from the movies: I'd been inspired by the film *Hoosiers* and touched by *Breaking Away*. At the time, I was unaware of the fact

that Indiana held the record for the state with the greatest
number of Ku Klux Klan lynchings of blacks. I soon discovered that Bedford was a community of blue-collar citizens
who made no effort to conceal the fact that African Americans were not welcome in their town. However, the time on
the job was quite enjoyable. When I made the transfer to
Bedford I found the forest supervisor, a white male, easy to
work with and very supportive of diversity. Within a few
months I was appointed diversity program manager as part
of my collaborative duties.

The supervisor respected me and accepted my recommendations. At the end of the first year in the position, I
received an outstanding performance rating and a quality
step increase award. According to the regional African
American Diversity Coordinator, I was the first African
American woman in the region to receive such an award.

However, in less than two years, this supervisor retired.
Then came the acting supervisor who wanted a "white only"
shop. He had no respect for women in general and African
American women in particular. To date, there is no African
American employed by the Hoosier National Forest. There is
one African American male housed in the building, but he is
employed by the Washington office. Through my years in that
office working for this supervisor, I applied numerous times
for a transfer, but to no avail. I soon became aware that I was
being blackballed, even though this fact was continuously
denied.

As you might expect, through the years snide and
unpleasant remarks were directed to me in meetings or
whenever the opportunity permitted. My supervisor
resented the fact that I have a relative who is an undersec-
retary in the government, and he used this on numerous
occasions to make unfair or cutting remarks; others did the
same. With a supportive supervisor, those remarks would
have been discredited. However, when the supervisor
became the leader of disparaging remarks, there is very little that can be done to dissuade others. I was consistently
and continuously the object of such behavior. If and when I
spoke up and expressed my displeasure with this type of
treatment it made bad matters worse.

Working with this supervisor soon became so stressful
that my health began to deteriorate. I went to work daily

feeling as though I was walking to my death, constantly
faced with defending myself in situations where I had little—and in some instance no—input. That was no life for
anyone to have to endure. Finally, I followed department
guidelines and filed a complaint with EEOC. However, that
action only exacerbated an already unbearable situation.

The lies and assumptions were too much to handle.
Neither my supervisor nor any other member of the Hoosier
Strategy Team took responsibility for their actions; in fact,
they attempted to lay any and all blame at my feet. I was
the only African American in leadership and I had no real
voice. Consequently, after months of pain and agony, and
having been diagnosed as suffering with a spastic colon
from stress, I decided the best thing for my peace of mind
and to improve my health was to resign. Currently, as I said
previously, Hoosier Forest is all white; the supervisor got
what he wanted.

In May 1996, I resigned and returned to my home in
New Mexico at my expense. I not only lost my job benefits
from the eight years; I had lost my good reputation as an
outstanding employee.

In June 1997, I was more or less forced to accept what
the Forest Service offered. As you probably know, one is
sworn to secrecy regarding settlements. I can understand
why that action is necessary: If I were the person responsible
for destroying another person's life and reputation through
falsehoods and institutional racism, I, too, would be ashamed
to be associated with this action! Not one person on the
Hoosier National Forest who was involved in helping to
destroy my life and reputation has been held accountable.
Nor has anyone been transferred because of his actions; it's
business as usual. They go along happily in their day-to-day
activities while I have been slandered.

I know the Department of Agriculture secretary sent
out numerous memos instructing the regional supervisors to
find a speedy resolution to the numerous complaints. However, management at lower levels continues to force and
intimidate ex-employees to "get it over with" and to accept
mediocre settlements. Now at age 52, I am again attending
the university in an attempt to prepare myself to compete
in this youth-oriented job market. I know I could have
refused the settlement offer; however, I was so sick of the

lies that were associated with my name, I had to get out from under it as quickly as possible.

Mr. President, I sincerely hope this letter gives you a little insight into what it's like to be an African American female in the Forest Service. Just check the statistics in the agency—the record speaks for itself. As your former Secretary of Agriculture stated, "it's time to close down the plantation known as the Forest Service." Please contact me if you would like additional information.

The best of luck to you in all your endeavors.


Respectfully,


Cheryl Boulden


cc:  National Task Force on Race Relations
     Rep. Albert R. Wynn
     Rep. Elijah E. Cummings


# DISCUSSION

1.  If you were appointed human resources representative for Hoosier National Forest, how would you go about investigating the allegations made by former-employee Cheryl Boulden?

2.  What approach would you take to make Hoosier National Forest's affirmative action plan more effective?

3.  What type of employee development and training plan would you draw up for the managers, supervisors, and employees of Hoosier National Forest?

# 13

## SEXUAL HARASSMENT

# Jailhouse Follies

*It is not always clear what actually constitutes "sexual harassment" and how it differs from other forms of discrimination based on sex or gender. Sometimes what is called sexual harassment by one person might be considered by another to be a simple case of bad manners, immaturity, or simply ignorance. There also are the cultural dimensions of sexual harassment as well—consider that in many cultures the concept of sexual harassment is simply unknown or not recognized. In the United States, sexual harassment is a major issue in the workplace, but there is no consensus regarding how it is defined or whether it was intended by the harasser.*

## BACKGROUND

There isn't much that's distinctive about Curry County, New Mexico, even when compared to other counties along the eastern part of the state, which the rest of New Mexico somewhat derisively refers to as "Little Texas." Clovis, county seat of Curry County, probably is most famous in the state as the city whose high school football teams have won more state titles in 4-AAAA football than any other high school—much to the chagrin of Albuquerque's more sophisticated residents. At least neighboring and much larger Roswell has the distinction of being known as the "alien capital" of the United States.

One of the best of the Clovis High School Wildcats' football teams won the state championship and went undefeated in 1989. Quarterbacking this group of kids was a fiery competitor by the name of Tomas Corona. However, Corona's moment of glory ended with high school graduation and marriage to his high school sweetheart. Upon graduation, Corona joined the Marines and spent four years away from Clovis. When discharged, Corona returned to Clovis with his family and to look for a job. Reluctantly, on January 1, 1993, Corona accepted a job that few other people wanted—as a detention officer at the Curry County Jail.

Quite surprisingly, Corona's career as a detention officer developed nicely and Corona received two promotions, the last to the rank of lieutenant on May 30, 1993. Lt. Corona found that he enjoyed the camaraderie of his coworkers at the jail and the position of respect and authority that it afforded; it reminded him of the good times he had enjoyed playing football and with his buddies in the Marine Corps.

However, Lt. Corona's world started to unravel in 1995–96 with a series of incidents involving alleged sexual harassment that would ultimately lead to his discharge as a lieutenant on August 13, 1996. This series of events would seriously divide the city of Clovis into two warring camps: (1) those who believed Lt. Corona was set up and wrongfully accused of sexual harassment, and (2) those where were convinced that Lt. Corona was guilty of sexual harassment. Coincidentally, critics of Lt. Corona were largely Caucasian and supporters were primarily Hispanic citizens.

The county's basis for discharge was based on the following four incidents of alleged misconduct and inappropriate behavior by Lt. Corona:

- *May 2, 1995.* Lt. Corona was informed by Don Bunson, director of the Curry County Detention Center (CCDC), that two female officers, Norma Niccolo and Florence Oropresa, would be assigned to his shift and supervision beginning on Monday of the following week. Lt. Corona did not know these officers at the time and expressed the following reservations to Director Bunson: "What about the capabilities of these female officers to restrain potentially violent inmates; will they be able to perform as well as male officers in similar circumstances?" Director Bunson emphasized that Officers Oropresa and Niccolo were well trained and should be given every opportunity to prove themselves. Lt. Corona later testified at his grievance hearing that he now believes that Officers Niccolo and Oropresa would be able to handle difficult inmates as well as male officers and he has total confidence in their abilities. At no time did Lt. Corona express any reservations directly to Officers Niccolo and Oropresa. Director Bunson entered the following notation in the supervisor's log for Lt. Corona on May 2, 1995: "Discussed importance of Female Officers." This entry was not shown to Lt. Corona until during the subsequent discovery process for the grievance hearing.

• *March 25, 1996.* Lt. Corona was verbally reprimanded by Director Bunson because of his comments made to Lt. Rosa Wortman regarding an incident that had previously occurred between Officer Jana Chambers and an inmate. Lt. Corona and Officer Pete Castillo had served on an Inmate Review Board and found an inmate not guilty of violating a rule in his behavior toward Officer Chambers. Specifically, Officer Chambers had asked the inmate, who was making a telephone call before dinner, when he was going to come, and the inmate had responded, "whenever you want me to." Officer Chambers wrote up the inmate for making a sexually explicit remark. However, the Review Board found that the inmate's comment was too vague to say with certainty that it was sexual in nature. Following this decision, Lt. Wortman confronted Lt. Corona because she strongly disagreed with the Review Board's decision. In response, Lt. Corona asked Lt. Wortman if Officer Chambers had done something to encourage the inmate to respond in an inappropriate manner. Lt. Wortman was offended by Corona's "sexist" question and reported it to Director Bunson, who subsequently reprimanded Lt. Corona. On March 25, 1996, Director Bunson entered the following statement regarding Lt. Corona into the supervisor's log, "Counseling for sexual harassment statement to Rosa about Jana." Director Bunson also sent a memo to Lt. Corona stating, "You are verbally reprimanded for being insensitive to the feelings of Officer Jana Chambers and Lt. Rosa Wortman during the discussion of disciplinary action against one of the inmates in a sexually motivated incident. This was explained to you as being sexual harassment and again you were told that this would not be tolerated from any employee of the County."

- *May 24, 1996*. Lt. Corona was in the booking area with several prisoners and Officer Sue Fenn when he observed Officer Fenn engaged in an animated conversation or dispute with her son. Officer Fenn subsequently remarked to Lt. Corona that her son was driving her crazy. Lt. Corona turned to her and said, "Look, quit your bitching. If you didn't want children, you shouldn't have spread your legs." Officer Fenn turned around and looked at Lt. Corona and said, "I can't believe you said that." Lt. Corona replied, "Come on, I'm just kidding around." Officer Fenn slapped Lt. Corona, who then ordered her to go home; however, Officer Fenn refused to do so and remained until Director Bunson arrived.

Lt. Corona subsequently received a seven-day suspension without pay and Officer Fenn was given a four-day suspension without pay. Lt. Corona's suspension letter included the following admonishment: "Your statement to Officer Fenn is completely unacceptable in a professional work environment. I have counseled you twice before about making statements that female employees might take offense to. You are given seven (7) days suspension without pay and a written reprimand in an attempt to make you more aware that this type of action is not acceptable."

- *July 26, 1996*. The culminating event that gave rise to Lt. Corona's discharge occurred on July 26 during a briefing of swing-shift employees in which Lt. Corona and Lt. Wortman were both sitting at the same desk completing paperwork. Lt. Corona was sitting directly in front of the desk and Lt. Wortman was working at the side; both were observed by Officer Randy McDonald. Officer McDonald said that he observed Lt. Corona "gently rub his foot across Lt. Wortman's bottom as she was seated at the desk." However, Lt. Wortman did not recall the incident or feel Lt. Corona's foot. Lt. Corona strongly denied that the incident ever occurred. Following this alleged incident, Lt. Wortman got up out of her chair and was moving it behind Lt. Corona to the other side, when Lt. Corona moved to stretch and touched Lt. Wortman on the left breast as she walked behind him. Lt. Corona does not deny that he touched Lt. Wortman, but claims it was accidental.

Officer McDonald observed the incident and testified that it appeared to be intentional and Lt. Corona had a smirk on his face; Officer McDonald was accused by Lt. Corona of lying for reasons unknown to him.

Director Bunson conducted an investigation of the incident. Following consideration of all the statements that he had collected during the investigation, Director Bunson presented the following memo to Lt. Corona in the disciplinary predetermination hearing: "It was reported to me that on the previous day's briefing of swing shift you were both rubbing your foot across Lt. Wortman's bottom and did place your hand on her breast. You attempted to make this last action appear to be an accident, but the opinion of the officer who was a witness felt it was deliberate. This type of disrespect for other employees of the Curry County Detention Center can no longer be tolerated."

## THE DECISION TO DISCHARGE

Following notification of impending charges by Director Bunson and the opportunity for Lt. Corona to respond in a predetermination hearing, County Manager Geneve Collins concluded that the preponderance of evidence supported Lt. Corona's dismissal because of the four incidents of sexual harassment. The county manager, after reviewing county policies and training for employees regarding sexual harassment—including that for Lt. Corona, found the following documentation:

• Curry County has clear and unambiguously stated policies prohibiting sexual harassment of employees by other employees. Included within the definition of sexual harassment is conduct that "has the purpose of affecting or unreasonably interfering with an individual's work performance or creating an intimidating, hostile, or offensive working environment." Curry County also has a policy statement indicating that it prohibits sexual harassment, and employees who commit offensive behavior are subject to disciplinary action. County employees are also encouraged to report acts of sexual harassment to the county manager or county attorney.

• Lt. Corona attended a sexual harassment training seminar on February 17, 1994, that was conducted by Darlene Gedritis of the New Mexico Association of Counties; Corona also attended a sexual harassment seminar on May 24, 1996, that was conducted by Paul Strokes of the New Mexico Department of Labor.

• All CCDC employees were warned in writing by Bunson on March 29, 1996, that sexual harassment would not be tolerated and that harassers would be subject to disciplinary action. All county employees were instructed in writing by Collins on May 22, 1996, to report all acts of sexual harassment to her.

• Several witnesses reported during the investigation that both male and female employees would occasionally participate in remarks and jokes of a sexual nature.

Based on the aforementioned evidence, the county manager imposed a discharge on Lt. Corona, who appealed the decision to a hearing officer for final review.

## THE DECISION TO DEMOTE

Under county personnel procedures, a hearing officer is selected to conduct an evidentiary hearing and make a final decision regarding whether disciplinary action was imposed for just cause. On January 17, 1997, the hearing officer conducted an evidentiary hearing that was attended by over 100 employees, friends, and relatives of those involved in this case. Following a review of the evidence and testimony, the hearing officer issued a report that included the following Conclusions of Law and decision:

### Conclusions of Law

1.    The county did not demonstrate through the preponderance of evidence admitted at the grievance hearing that Lt. Corona was guilty of sexual harassment on May 2, 1995, when he objected to the assignment of female officers to his shift and supervision. This discussion occurred between

Director Bunson and Lt. Corona and was not relayed to the female officers. Lt. Corona expressed an opinion to his supervisor, one that he no longer holds. These comments were uninformed at the time, but one cannot reasonably conclude that they constituted harassment of female employees or contributed to a "hostile work environment."

2. The county did not demonstrate through the preponderance of evidence admitted at the hearing that Lt. Corona was guilty of sexual harassment on March 25, 1996, when he asked Lt. Wortman if Officer Chambers had done anything to provoke the inmate's response. Lt. Corona did not initiate the conversation with Lt. Wortman or speak directly with Officer Chambers. The remarks reflect possible gender stereotyping and insensitivity, but one cannot reasonably conclude that Lt. Corona sexually harassed Officer Chambers when he responded to Lt. Wortman's confrontational questioning.

3. The county demonstrated through the preponderance of evidence admitted at the hearing that Lt. Corona was guilty of sexual harassment on May 24, 1996, when he made an offensive comment to Officer Fenn, which provoked her immediate and physical response. Lt. Corona's comment was demeaning and derogatory of women; it contributed to a hostile work environment. Lt. Corona's action was mitigated slightly by indications that Officer Fenn and others participated in comments and actions that were sexual in nature.

4. The county demonstrated through the preponderance of evidence admitted at the hearing that Lt. Corona was guilty of sexual harassment on July 26, 1996, when his hand touched Lt. Wortman's breast as she walked behind him. It is uncontested that the action occurred and one must reasonably conclude that it was intentional, based on the disinterested testimony of Officer McDonald. However, the county did not conclusively demonstrate that Lt. Corona sexually harassed Lt. Wortman by intentionally touching her bottom. Lt. Wortman did not know if she had been touched and only complained of this action after she was told by Officer McDonald that it had occurred. Although Lt. Corona possibly touched Lt. Wortman's bottom, as testified to by Officer McDonald, it cannot be conclusively determined that his touch was intentional.

5. Conclusions reached regarding the incident of July 26 hinge largely on witness credibility, specifically the

corroborating testimony of Officer McDonald, who was admittedly reluctant to "get involved" and only did so when ordered by Director Bunson. Clearly, this witness had no conflict of interest of apparent motive to give damaging testimony against Lt. Corona. Thus, his testimony corroborates the credible testimony already given by Lt. Wortman.

## Decision

After considering the testimony and listening to the arguments presented by the parties, the hearing officer for Curry County found that on two occasions Lt. Corona committed wrongdoing that constituted sexual harassment of female employees. His behavior on those two occasions is only partially mitigated by past workplace behavior in the CCDC.

Even though Lt. Corona is guilty of wrongdoing, discharge is overly punitive in this matter. Even so, Lt. Corona as a supervisor and manager is required to adhere to a higher standard of behavior and serve as a role model for subordinates. His immature and inappropriate actions indicate that he has not accepted a higher level of responsibility implicit in supervisory and managerial positions.

The hearing officer ordered that Lt. Corona be reinstated and demoted from lieutenant to the rank of detention officer with full back pay, benefits, and seniority as a detention officer to his date of discharge.

## DISCUSSION

1.  To what extent do you agree with the county's position that it had just cause to discharge Lt. Corona for four incidents of sexual harassment?

2.  To what extent do you agree with the hearing officer's conclusion that Lt. Corona was guilty of only two incidents of sexual harassment?

3.  In terms of these incidents, discuss (1) intended and unintended harassment, (2) gender stereotyping, and (3) creation of a hostile work environment.

# 14

## ETHNIC DISCRIMINATION

# Culture Clash at the Cancer Center

*I'm not used to working with lazy Mexicans. You know
how those people are; they're always thinking about siestas. So nothing gets done on time because it's mañana,
mañana.*

—*Indrit Khalsa*

Susan Finn, associate director of human resources at the Eastern New Mexico Medical Center (ENMMC) in Roswell, was
deeply perplexed and uncertain of what to do next. Over the
past several months, all six staff members of Radiation Oncology had come to Finn separately with complaints regarding
alleged abusive behavior exhibited by a contract physician,
Indrit Khalsa, and directed toward Hispanic and female staff
as well as patients. Specifically, a number of staff members
presented Finn with the following complaints, which they were
reluctant to put in writing for fear of retaliation by ENMMC
management, who they believed did not wish to jeopardize the
revenues that Dr. Khalsa brought into the ENMMC:

• *Pat Chavez*, an experienced dosimetrist with 20 years'
experience, who complained that Khalsa frequently referred
to Hispanics as "those people who are lazy and dirty." After
one particularly derogatory remark about Juan Sanchez,

Chavez confronted Khalsa and asked him not to make these remarks, but Khalsa simply ignored him.

• *Betty Cabeza de Baca*, licensed practical nurse, had been the brunt of numerous tirades and abusive remarks by Khalsa. On one occasion, when de Baca had momentarily forgotten in which room she had left a patient, Khalsa erupted, "You're so stupid. You can't even remember where you put the patient; all you think about is taking siestas." On another occasion Khalsa had told a head nurse not to let Betty treat an affluent white patient, "because she is not of her kind." Khalsa informed another patient who offered him a tamale, "You make that out of the insides of a pig, and I don't eat junk like that, but you can give it to her [Betty] if you like." But the final straw occurred when Khalsa informed Betty's daughter, Contessa, that she would never be tall: "You're going to be a short little Mexican."

• *Anna Maria Murieta*, a young tech assistant, who helped the technicians prepare patients and their setups, was also upset with Dr. Khalsa's behavior, but did not want to risk losing the only steady job she had held since graduating from high school five years ago.

• *Sandra Newhouse*, a radiation oncology nurse, stated that Khalsa had belittled staff in front of patients and was breaching patient confidentiality from one patient to another. Newhouse indicated that on one occasion Khalsa had told one patient that another was also undergoing experimental high-dose chemotherapy treatment for lymphoma, but her prognosis was not good.

Finn listened sympathetically when these employees had sought her out to complain about Khalsa's behavior toward them as well as toward poor, female, and Hispanic patients.

The complaining employees were particularly incensed when Khalsa would not drape these women during examinations. He also would sometimes pinch the patients' nipples or pop the patients with his finger during examinations, but he claimed this was a necessary part of the process. Despite Khalsa's objectionable behavior, Finn had been repeatedly instructed by her boss, Jeff McKeleher, the vice president for human resources, not to investigate these complaints unless they were put in writing. McKeleher explained that Finn should leave relations with the physicians up to him and just handle the staff side of things. Besides, McKeleher assured her, he would make certain that all the complaints she relayed to him were given to top management at the ENMMC.

Over the next several months, Khalsa's behavior became even more abusive, and several staff members began to apply for positions outside of Radiology Oncology. Finn was dubious that her concerns regarding Khalsa's behavior ever left Mc-Keleher's office. Finally, Finn confronted McKeleher and demanded to know what he had done about the situation with Khalsa and if Finn's concerns even had been delivered to ENMMC management. McKeleher became very agitated and told Finn to mind staff affairs and let him handle physicians. After all, McKeleher warned, these physicians are not regular employees of ENMMC and serve on a contractual basis: "You know we really can't do anything about them and staff is expendable; so just don't rock the boat."

Finally, Finn decided she could no longer ignore the problems and needed documentation to protect herself should there be subsequent litigation. Thus, Finn prepared the following memo for Dr. Tristani, vice president of medical affairs:

It has been brought to my attention by the staff of the Department of Radiation Oncology that they are concerned about what they consider inappropriate behavior toward them by Dr. Khalsa. Their complaints echo of direct verbal abuse, gender discrimination, racially inflammatory remarks, breach of patient confidentiality, and unprofessionalism. Discussion with employees indicates that this behavior is continuing to worsen as patient volumes increase. In the past months, both Pat Chavez and I have talked with Dr. Khalsa about anti-Hispanic comments made in the public areas of the department, but with no success. Nor have my mediation attempts yielded any positive change in his behavior. The female staff members and one male staff member state that they are continually subjected to fits of anger and verbal reprimands by Dr. Khalsa in front of the patients and other staff, whereas male staff are not treated in a derogatory manner. I have discussed this with male employees and they are in complete agreement. Dr. Khalsa has also been seen to throw consent forms and charts at Betty Cabeza de Baca when he doesn't like the work she has done. On another occasion, his anger at Anna Maria Murieta was so great that she could no longer perform her job responsibilities and had to go home for the remainder of the day. As you are aware, there has been a significant amount of turnover in the Radiation Oncology Department. At the present time, I believe we have recruited a very good staff of therapists and nurses. They are working diligently to become a cohesive department that provides compassionate quality care for their patients. Because they are new to ENMMC, and they are from different backgrounds, this will take a little time. They are willing to work with Dr. Khalsa, but not under these circumstances.

Please let me know as soon as possible how you intend to handle this matter.

Thank you.

The following morning, Finn received a call from Tristani's secretary that she was expected to be in Tristani's office within the hour to meet with Khalsa; and the secretary confided, "And he's not a very happy camper!"

## DISCUSSION

1.  To whom, if anyone, should Finn have sent copies of her memo to Tristani?

2.  You are Tristani, and Finn's memo comes as a complete surprise to you. How would you respond to Finn? Khalsa? McKeleher?

3.  You are Finn. What documentation do you take with you to the appointment with Tristani? Who, if anyone, would you telephone prior to the meeting with Tristani?

# 15

## OFF-DUTY CONDUCT

# The Cop and
# the Prostitute

*In a romantic comedy film of 1963 directed by Billy Wilder,* Irma La Douce, *Jack Lemmon plays a Parisian gendarme whose well-ordered beat is upset by a prostitute, acted by Shirley MacLaine. In Hollywood, the end is somewhat romantic and cute; in the real world, cops and prostitutes are a highly problematic mixture.*

Detective Sergeant Chuck Ferrel of the Albuquerque Police Department (APD) was completing his third tour of duty in the Internal Affairs Division, and he hated these types of cases more than any others—investigating cops who screwed up in their private lives so that the department got a lot of bad publicity. It was particularly bad when the cop was a supervisor and otherwise an excellent officer. And Sergeant Sergio Guzman fit that description, even to the point of recently having been awarded the department's Medal of Meritorious Service for his bravery in saving the life of a fellow officer during a drug bust gone bad.

To make matters worse, this would be the second time in the last three years that Sgt. Ferrel had been given the assignment of conducting an internal affairs investigation into Sgt. Guzman's relationship with Penny O'Laughlin, a reported addict and prostitute. Sergeant Ferrel knew that his investigation and follow-up report—as it had in 1995—would again play a major role in the likely decision by police brass regarding how severely to discipline Sgt. Guzman. Sergeants Ferrel and Guzman had gone through the academy together, and Sgt. Ferrel did not look forward to the distasteful job ahead of him.

## THE 1995 INCIDENT

First, Sgt. Ferrel reviewed the Internal Affairs Investigation Report in 1995 that spelled out the not-too-pretty tale of Sgt. Guzman's relationship with O'Laughlin:

• In 1991, Sgt. Guzman had been working vice when he apprehended O'Laughlin working as a prostitute along Central Avenue near Louisiana, in an infamous red-light district. Suspecting that O'Laughlin was also involved in a drug trafficking ring, Sgt. Guzman persuaded O'Laughlin to work as a decoy in a trap to catch the ringleaders, who were vicious criminals recently resettled from Cuba.

• From 1991 through 1995, Sgt. Guzman and O'Laughlin pursued a social relationship that eventually became intimate in nature. Sgt. Guzman would help O'Laughlin out of trouble and support her through periodic stays in detox centers as she tried to kick her drug addiction; Sgt. Guzman would allow O'Laughlin's six-year-old son sometimes to stay with him, and he had tried to assist O'Laughlin by occasionally assisting with her four-year-old child, even though neither of these children was his.

• Sgt. Guzman said that on one occasion he did not hear from O'Laughlin, after loaning her his car to do errands on a Friday afternoon, until Monday night around 2100 hours, "when she just appeared at my door, without my car, and wanted to come inside." Sergeant Guzman recounted, "I did not let her into my house and told her to go to a shelter." However, O'Laughlin stayed at his door for the next several hours and begged him to let her in. Finally, Sgt. Guzman stated he called his lieutenant, Gil Nadia, when O'Laughlin refused to leave. After this call, O'Laughlin did leave for a period of time, but eventually returned that night, crying and pleading with him to let her in. She said she was freezing, so Sgt. Guzman gave her a couple of blankets and told her she needed to find someplace else to go. O'Laughlin continued to plead with him, so Sgt. Guzman called the rescue van to come and pick her up. Eventually the van did arrive and took O'Laughlin to the Joy Junction Shelter. Sgt. Guzman told Ferrel that O'Laughlin called him the next day and that he told her that he could no longer help her out in any way.

- On June 28, 1995, Sgt. Guzman contacted Lt. Ramos, his supervisor, at her home while off duty, to complain that he found O'Laughlin at his house and could not persuade her to leave. As a consequence, the Domestic Abuse Response Team (DART) responded and took O'Laughlin away; both Sgt. Guzman and O'Laughlin were ordered not to contact each other. Subsequently, Sgt. Guzman met with Capt. Cordera and Lt . Ramos, who advised Sgt. Guzman to stay away from O'Laughlin. However, Sgt. Guzman was not given a direct order, either in writing or verbally, not to see O'Laughlin.

- In 1995, Sgt. Guzman picked up O'Laughlin and dropped her off at an apartment complex, ostensibly to pick up several things from her girlfriend, while Sgt. Guzman waited outside in the car. O'Laughlin returned to the car and they left. Unknown to Sgt. Guzman and O'Laughlin, the same complex was under surveillance by undercover police officers, who traced the vehicle as belonging to Sgt. Guzman. Sgt. Guzman was subsequently disciplined with a 40-hour suspension without pay for violations of Standard Operating Procedures (SOP) 1-04-1, "Personal Code of Conduct," and 1-04-6, "Conduct Both On and Off Duty" (see below).

- Once again, Sgt. Guzman was under investigation by Internal Affairs because of his personal relationship with O'Laughlin, and it was Sgt. Ferrel's assignment to conduct the investigation. The incidents initiating the current investigation occurred off duty on November 15, 16, and 17, 1996.

Preliminarily, Sgt. Guzman was believed by the department to have committed violations of the following SOPs and it was Sgt. Ferrel's task to determine if, indeed, violations had occurred:

- 1-04-1 PERSONAL CODE OF CONDUCT

  (G). Conduct unbecoming an officer or employee shall include:
    (1). That which could bring the department into disrepute; or
    (2). That which impairs the operation or efficiency of the department.

- 1-04-4 CONDUCT WHILE ON DUTY

  (J). Insubordination consists of any employee who:
    (1). Willfully neglects or deliberately refuses any lawful order given by a superior and/or acting supervisor. . . .

- 1-04-6 CONDUCT BOTH ON AND OFF DUTY

  (C). Personnel shall avoid regular or continuous associations with persons whom they know are under active criminal investigation or indictment, or who have a reputation in the community or the department for present involvement in felonious or criminal behavior, except as necessary in the performance of official duties, or where unavoidable because of other personal relationships.

## THE 1996–97 INVESTIGATION

Sgt. Ferrel conducted extensive interviews of numerous individuals over the next two months and compiled the following "factual basis for discipline":

- On November 17, 1996, Sgt. Guzman reported that his personal vehicle was not returned by O'Laughlin after he loaned it to her to go to work on November 14, 1996. On November 16, 1996, Sgt. Guzman's vehicle, while in the possession of O'Laughlin, was listed as a suspect vehicle in a commercial burglary.

- O'Laughlin has an extensive criminal history of charges involving drug use, trafficking, theft, and prostitution. However, only one of these charges resulted in an actual conviction, and there was no current felony investigation. Sgt. Guzman admitted he was aware of O'Laughlin's reputation at the time he was previously disciplined for his involvement with her.

• When interviewed by Sgt. Ferrel, Sgt. Guzman stated that he loaned O'Laughlin his car so that she could get to work and that she had agreed to bring the car back after work that night. (She worked as a waitress at a neighborhood pub, The Gin Mill.) When O'Laughlin had not returned the car by the following morning, Sgt. Guzman then filed the report of an embezzled car.

• Then Sgt. Guzman dropped his bombshell to Ferrel. Sgt. Guzman added that O'Laughlin had been staying at his house since the last part of July 1996 even though he'd gotten in trouble once before because of her visit to drug dealers; O'Laughlin was staying there because he and O'Laughlin have a baby daughter together, and this was the reason for continuing the relationship with O'Laughlin. Sgt. Guzman said, "I wanted to make a good life for my baby as well as help Penny in getting her life straightened out so that she could provide for the baby." Sgt. Guzman stated he found out O'Laughlin was pregnant at approximately the same time he was being disciplined in the first Internal Affairs case regarding this matter. Sgt. Guzman, feeling a responsibility to help raise the child and because of O'Laughlin's high-risk pregnancy, allowed O'Laughlin to move into his house. O'Laughlin stayed in Guzman's house until the premature delivery; the baby's fragile condition did not allow release from the hospital until mid-October 1996. Guzman stated that he mentioned that O'Laughlin was pregnant to only one person, Lt. Nadia.

• Sgt. Ferrel was flabbergasted and asked, "Don't you remember getting a verbal directive from Lt. Ramos and Capt. Cordera to discontinue seeing O'Laughlin?" Sgt. Guzman replied, "Well I don't recall being ordered to stay away from O'Laughlin; their advice was something informal between friends. I've always had a good working relationship with Capt. Cordera and Lt. Ramos and I felt it was advice coming from friends." Sgt. Guzman did not remember signing any directive or order, other than the final notice of discipline he received in early 1996.

• Deputy Chief Burgess had imposed a 40-hour suspension in 1995, rather than a more severe penalty, because he was convinced that Sgt. Guzman would end his relationship with O'Laughlin. However, Deputy Chief Burgess did not give Sgt. Guzman a direct order, either verbally or in writing, to cease his contact with O'Laughlin.

As the final part of his investigation, Sgt. Ferrel decided to interview O'Laughlin, whom he met in a cheap rooming house downtown. O'Laughlin was despondent over the fact that Sgt. Guzman had imposed a restraining order to keep her from harassing him and their daughter, of whom he now had sole custody. The following dialogue between Sgt. Ferrel and O'Laughlin transpired:

**O'L:** I should have left a long time ago. I really love that guy. I should have left a long time ago, to not jeopardize his career.

**Ferrel:** Are you going to accuse him of anything?

**O'L:** I have nothing to say about him except for that he's a very good man. People see me as a druggie and a whore, but when I was with him, I was straight.

**Ferrel:** Is there anything else you'd like to comment on?

**O'L:** Nothing. I just pray to God that he's not in trouble because of this. And if there's anything I can do, please let me know, OK?

**Ferrel:** Well, it's a difficult thing for us to do, to investigate one of our own officers.

**O'L:** He does not deserve to be investigated. I do. I just want to know what's going to happen to him? He's a very good guy. You know, people have problems. And there's been other cops out here that have offered to help. And you know all they want is a piece of ass, right? No, this guy really cares and he wants to help. Do you now how many cops out there date hookers and they do this and do that? He's not like that. So why is this finger being pointed at him?

Sgt. Ferrel concluded his investigation, with the reluctant realization that he would be compelled by the facts to find that Sgt. Guzman had violated each of the departmental SOPs, as charged.

# DISCUSSION

1.  State the reasons why you would either agree or disagree with Sgt. Ferrel's decision to find Sgt. Guzman guilty of violating departmental SOPs?

2.  If you were either Lt. Ramos or Capt. Cordera, how would you have handled the situation with Sgt. Ramos following the 1995 incident at the apartment complex?

3.  To what extent should public employers be allowed to regulate off-duty behavior of employees, particularly police officers, without intruding upon an employee's constitutional right to privacy?

# 16

## EMPLOYEE DATING AND PRIVACY

# The Case of the Cuddly Custodian

*Incline Village, Nevada, is increasingly called "Income Village" because billionaires are buying out millionaires and paying top dollar for prime Lake Tahoe lakefront property and building their dream homes. Upscale beach homes owned by well-to-do people are nothing new in this town of about 9,000, on the east shore of one of the world's clearest and deepest high-altitude lakes.*

Lynn R. Simpson is curriculum coordinator and coordinator of staff training for the Washoe County School District in Nevada. She is frequently called upon to conduct training in gender discrimination and, specifically, how to investigate sexual harassment complaints. During the first week of May 1997, Simpson was engaged in training at Incline Elementary School (E.S.) in Incline Village regarding sexual harassment. Following the first session of her training, several teachers took her aside and made complaints of sexual harassment against Thomas Canden, the head custodian at their school.

As a result, Simpson went to Incline E.S. on May 30 and met with Principal Ed Henry and Cathy Wadell, a teacher; Simpson subsequently interviewed a former teacher, Karen Landry, who had also complained separately to Tom Strauss in the district's personnel office. Based on her conversation,

Simpson later spoke with Principal Henry, secretary Liz Herrera, and teachers Kenna Jones, Mary Osmond, Kim Warfield, Melissa Farve, Cathy Cecilli, and Molly Blue on June 7. Karen Landry was not interviewed but agreed to send a letter instead, which described her encounters with Canden. Simpson also interviewed Diana Barnes, a custodian who had worked directly for Canden.

Simpson used a matrix when interviewing these women to determine if the incidents described met criteria for determining whether Canden had committed sexual harassment by his actions. The matrix posed four questions to the interviewees regarding Canden's behavior:

• Was it sexual in nature/gender-related?
• Was it unwelcome or unwanted?
• Was it severe/pervasive in impact?
• Did it interfere with work (did it make you feel differently about being at work?).

Simpson's matrix indicated that the incidents involving Wadell, Landry, and Barnes met all four criteria while the encounters with Osmond and Herrera met two or three criteria. Simpson was also aware that the district's sexual harassment policy had been presented at orientation for new employees and posted at school sites. In addition, a March 21, 1997, training for sexual harassment at Incline E.S. was offered. Canden had gone to part of the training and later attended a make-up session in Reno in April 1997. Formal investigation started on May 30, 1997. Investigators Simpson and Strauss interviewed the aggrieved individuals and reported the following facts:

## KAREN LANDRY

Landry had been a music teacher for ten years, formerly at Incline E.S. (1990–1991 to 1994–1995). Landry wrote a letter to Strauss following sexual harassment training in March 1996 because only then did she realize how angry and upset she still was because of Canden's behavior. Landry stated that "I was an emotional basket case. Canden joined the staff in

April/May of '94, and I thought we had a professional relation-ship, until the summer when he said, 'Gee that's a nice pair of legs and I'd really like to be between them.' I was really upset."

Landry's next contact with Canden came early in the school year when he violated her personal space by stand-ing so close that she had to back up to the wall. "I was very upset because he wanted to go out on a date." The next inci-dent was prior to setting up for the Christmas program dress rehearsal; Landry needed custodial help with risers and equipment. Landry asked Canden, "Would you come in the morning?" and he said, "Well that depends on if there's anyone around." In February, Canden handed Landry his personal card and said they would be a "hot item" and he was volunteering "stud service." "I didn't say anything immediately because I depended on custodians and must work closely with them. I altered my behavior to avoid him as much as possible; I took every single day of sick leave. I decided to transfer out because I knew that I couldn't han-dle this problem even though I had to sell my home at a loss. I was on Prozac and taking meds for asthma, hormones, and such." Sometimes Landry would sit in a room alone crying because of the way Canden treated her; Landry stated, "I felt like he was verbally slapping me around" and that "Other men have complimented me but none made me feel vulgar."

Landry admitted that she never told Canden, "I'm offended by your words," but she did report them to her prin-cipal at least four times. Landry indicated that she realized later that she should have been keeping notes throughout. There were no witnesses to any of the incidents. Landry stated that she should not have kept it inside and, if she had it to do over again, would have taken action much earlier.

## CATHY WADELL

Wadell was a young single parent and teacher at Incline E.S., who served as a student teacher beginning in August 1996. Canden approached her at the copier machine sometime dur-ing October or November 1996 and asked her for a date; he said, "We could have a drink or perhaps dinner." Wadell stated that she told him, "I am in love with my boyfriend and very committed." Wadell indicated to Simpson that she hoped this would end the matter and was very clear in her intent. Wadell revealed that soon afterward, Canden approached her in the cafeteria and asked if he could write her a letter: "He crouched over me so no one else could hear. I was angry, offended, it violated my space." Wadell told him, "Not if it's going to offend me." Wadell indicated that she was very uncomfortable because she had no idea when the letter would arrive.

Wadell did not have long to wait. The dreaded letter came a few days later when Canden hand-delivered it to her classroom without saying anything. Wadell indicated that the content of the letter's message was as follows:

- He knew I had a boyfriend and it was OK.
- He'd had a dream lately in which he had sex with me.
- He wanted a relationship with me and I had nice qualities.
- He would keep our relationship a secret.

Wadell stated that she initially was in shock and didn't read the letter a second time; she mulled it over for three days trying to decide what to do. Wadell indicated that she carried it around in her bag and couldn't sleep for two nights; nor did she tell her boyfriend about the letter.

Finally, after carrying the letter around for over a week, Wadell threw it in the trash, without keeping a copy. When probed by Simpson, Wadell admitted that she thought about going to the principal but she really wanted a teaching job at Incline E.S., and didn't want to be a troublemaker. When asked about the effects upon her relationship with Canden, she described it as totally changed: "I avoided him and I wouldn't use the copier in the basement near his office. I didn't ask for janitorial service." Wadell finished student teaching in December 1996 and accepted a teaching job that opened up in January 1997.

Sometime in March, Wadell went to secretary Liz Herrera to order a pencil sharpener because she didn't want contact with Canden; she told Herrera where it should be installed. After it was installed, Wadell indicated that Canden came to her room: "He walked past my desk with a smirk on his face and left without doing anything to the sharpener."

After the sexual harassment training workshop, Wadell felt uncomfortable and distraught. So she went to Herrera's office and all of her pent-up frustration came out unexpectedly. Herrera encouraged Wadell to tell Principal Henry, but she told another teacher instead. "I had a home in Incline and two small boys; my divorce became final in March 1996; and I was afraid."

## MARY OSMOND

Osmond, a teacher at Incline E.S., was working during the summer of 1995 on a non-school day. Osmond indicated that she was walking down the hall past a stairway when "Tom whistled at me in an inappropriate manner . . . a construction site whistle." Osmond stated that she didn't acknowledge it and wrote a letter of complaint to Principal Henry. Osmond later received a letter of apology in her office box from Canden.

A second incident happened when Custodian Alfredo was moving bulletin boards for Osmond. Canden saw him and reprimanded Alfredo; he took him off the job immediately and his tools with him. "We had to finish the job ourselves, even though Alfredo had initially been given approval by Tom to help us."

## MOLLY BLUE

Blue, a teacher at Incline E.S., recounted an incident with Canden that occurred during the fall of 1995, when she received a message on her home answering machine from Canden suggesting that they should get together. Blue was surprised because she hardly knew Canden. "Throughout the fall, he would give me flirtatious looks and once commented 'Nice legs.'" Blue began to keep her work requests for custodians to a minimum; she also didn't come to school at nights or on weekends.

The second incident occurred during 1996–97, outside work, at a hockey game that Blue attended with her girlfriend. They saw Canden and he later called Blue and wanted to know if her girlfriend was single.

## ELIZABETH HERRERA

Herrera had been the secretary at Incline E.S. for seven years. She recounted an incident that occurred in November 1996. Herrera had ordered a computer stand for her desk; when it arrived she discovered that the computer holder required brackets on her desk for a raised monitor. Canden came in and asked where the holder was and Herrera said, "It's in my box." Canden replied, "Oh that sounds like fun to look in to it." Herrera said, "Tom, knock it off!" As secretary, Herrera had daily interactions with Canden and observed him viewing females with an up-and-down stare. "He would stare at my chest, and when I bent over, it felt uncomfortable."

Herrera admitted that she frequently interacted with Principal Henry but never said anything to him about Canden. "When Cathy Wadell told me what had happened, I told her to see Henry."

## MELISSA FARVE

Farve, also a teacher at Incline E.S., stated that Canden made an inappropriate comment in late 1995 as she was walking down the hall and he was close by. "I turned to say hello and he made a comment regarding my appearance; he had a smirk on his face and he looked me up and down." Canden said something about Farve's hair style, suntan, and dress. "He gave me a very uncomfortable feeling and thereafter I chose not to go to school after work without my husband." Farve reported his comment to Principal Henry and another teacher, and Henry said he would take care of it.

## DIANA BARNES

Barnes, an attractive African American single parent, was formerly a custodian at Incline E.S.; she was now at another school. Barnes was a custodian at Incline E.S. when Canden became head custodian in 1995. Barnes told Simpson that Canden was "disrespectful, rude, and harsh; he used sexual language around me and mentioned women's crotches, breasts, and other body parts." Canden once told her that "he could have me within two years, meaning that I was weak and would go to bed with him." Canden constantly used "nasty talk." Barnes stated that she told Alfredo and he talked to Canden, and it seemed to stop somewhat. "I told Tom that I didn't want to hear that type of talk and Tom replied that I worked with guys and that's how they talked." Afterwards, Barnes left Incline E.S. and went to another school because "I felt trapped and didn't want to hear that kind of talk. I went to my association rep, and we went to the principal to complain. Later, Tom helped me find another school near Carson City where I wanted to move anyway."

## TOM CANDEN

Prior to his position as head custodian at Incline E.S., Canden had a long work history of managing roller rinks and servicing copier machines. Canden is 55 years old, overweight, and had never been accused of inappropriate behavior in managing employees. Canden has always had outstanding performance evaluations. He was first told of the accusations when Strauss called him in for an interview in June 1997. Canden had been active in singles groups in the past but is now happily married. Canden said, "I'm not aware that I looked at anyone inappropriately. No one counseled me that I might be disciplined in the future." Canden responded to the accusations against him as follows:

- *Karen Landry.* "I did say 'Hey, she's got legs' but did not say I'd like to get between them. I did not impose myself on her or try to date her. I did ask where singles meet in the area; she liked to talk to me because she couldn't talk to other teachers. Regarding the incident when she asked me to come in the morning—I asked if we were going to be alone but never laughed. She never told me not to talk about anything or said she was offended; I never retaliated or asked for sex. I did tell her that I wasn't going to ask her out, because we were on the same staff. I also never had a conversation with Henry regarding Karen."

- *Cathy Wadell.* Canden admitted that he sent a letter to Wadell, but only after asking her if he could give her a letter in the multipurpose room—to which she said "yes." "I was asking her out, but it was not a sexual dream. The letter said that I saw her in a dream, that she would be leaving in three days, and I wanted to ask her out for coffee. If your answer is no, you don't need to respond. I didn't want to embarrass her and didn't say anything about a boyfriend. We never discussed the letter again."

• *Mary Osmond.* "I had conversation with Henry regarding Mary Osmond because she was offended by the whistle, but I wrote a letter of apology; I was not aware that I'd received an oral reprimand from Henry, who told me to be more careful and apologize; I never whistled at her again."

• *Molly Blue.* "I didn't mean to offend Molly by calling her at home; I just wanted to meet her friend and I knew that we were both single."

• *Elizabeth Herrera.* "I told her that I could put in a computer between the legs of the table but it wasn't sexual and I never said it would be fun. I always thought we had a good working relationship; she never said anything to me about my remarks."

• *Melissa Farve.* "I was new to the school and just wanted to be friendly because I was the new custodian there. I was raised in the old school where men could compliment a woman when she looked good. I didn't mean to offend her."

• *Diana Barnes.* "I never said that I could have her in two years nor made remarks to her about crotches or breasts. I only saw her twice a week during the school year (she was on the night shift). Henry told me unofficially that Diana might file a grievance on me and gave me a copy of the sexual harassment policy but never warned me or said anything was improper."

Canden offered his point of view: "I know as a matter of common sense not to treat people in a sexually degrading way. I received a copy of the Sexual Harassment Policy, but I don't remember anyone discussing the policy with me." In Spring 1995, Canden stated that he printed up a personal card with attributes; he gave this card to Landry soon after meeting her, but denied ever telling her, "I'll give you all the action you'll ever want." Canden also put up a sign in front of his house, tacked on a tree, which said that he wanted to meet a woman and listed his personal attributes. Canden also denied that he ever asked Cathy Wadell out prior to sending her a letter. "If she had told me not to give her a letter, I would not have done so."

## DISCUSSION

1.  You are Lynn Simpson and are reviewing all the information that you've collected. You are trying to objectively assess the evidence against Canden. Where do you have a strong case and which areas still trouble you?

2.  You are Tom Strauss and are faced with making a recommendation to the district superintendent regarding Canden and Principal Henry. What are you going to recommend?

# 17

## EMPLOYEE DUE PROCESS

# Sergeant Preston of the Yukon Police

*In the early days of radio (prior to television), one of the more popular programs was about the adventures of Sergeant Preston of the Royal Canadian Mounted Police in the Yukon Territory of Canada, who, with his trustworthy dog "King," used to lead the fight for law and order in the desolate regions of the Polar North.*

As one enters Yukon, Oklahoma, a huge water tower sign announces that Yukon is the home town of famous country and western singer Garth Brooks. As might be expected, things are fairly predictable in Yukon, Oklahoma. For example, every May, graduating seniors from high school and middle school celebrate the end of the academic year by engaging in shaving cream fights in local parks. This year was no exception: Like clockwork, over a hundred middle school students gathered to engage in their annual ritual of baptism by shaving cream and water—under the watchful eye of several parents, including petite Sheila Janes, who, in her "hot pink" shorts, was having as much fun as the kids. At 11 A.M., when the kids were thoroughly covered with water and shaving cream, Roberta Morris drove by, only to be sprayed in the face as she slowed down to watch the spectacle. This did not make Morris a happy camper as she left and immediately called the police in order to register a complaint against the revelers.

Sgt. Robert Preston of the Yukon Police, working undercover in civilian clothes, responded to the call from the police dispatcher and went immediately to the scene of the incident. Sgt. Preston surveyed a veritable sea of kids in the park, who were covered with lather and soaking wet. Preston moved assertively near the center of the kids with his police vehicle, stopped, and ordered them to immediately disperse. Sheila Janes at this point objected, causing Preston to ask her to identify herself. However, Janes refused and Preston informed her that she could either produce identification or face arrest (even though he could not legally arrest a citizen for failing to give an ID under Oklahoma statute).

By this time, Morris had returned, whereupon she and Janes began a heated argument. Preston then told Janes that she was under arrest. Janes responded by turning away from Preston, and, walking toward the crowd, said, "Go to hell." (Janes would later claim that her words were not directed at Preston.) At this point, Sgt. Preston reached out and grabbed Janes by the arm, then leaned her over the hood of his vehicle as he clamped the handcuffs on one arm. Janes's children started crying and yelling at Preston to leave their mommy alone.

Preston, afraid that the situation could rapidly escalate out of his control, decided not to cuff Janes's other wrist and ordered her inside his vehicle, where he informed her that she had just been "unarrested," and that she needed to leave the scene immediately. Janes exited the police car, gathered up her kids, and left the scene. Preston later filed a police incident report and informed Chief of Police Harold Darby that he could probably expect a citizen complaint from Janes later in the day.

Sure enough, about an hour later, Janes came in with her kids to complain to Chief Darby and let him know that she fully intended to file a tort claim against the city because of Sgt. Preston's alleged use of unnecessary force on her. Chief Darby assured Janes that he would take appropriate action against Sgt. Preston and it would not be necessary for Janes to fill out an official citizen's complaint regarding the matter (as required by municipal ordinance). Chief Darby did not subsequently inform Preston of his conversation with Janes or meet again with Preston until months later. Even though members of the same department, Darby and Preston had a number of conflicts over the years stemming from Preston's former service as president of the local lodge of the Fraternal Order of Police; their relationship had particularly soured several years earlier when Chief Darby had given Preston the only disciplinary blemish on his personnel record—a letter of reprimand for not cleaning the engine of Preston's patrol vehicle.

Throughout June and the beginning of July, Preston assumed that the incident had been forgotten as he heard nothing more about it. That changed on July 14, when the city manager was served with notice that Sheila Janes had indeed filed a tort claim in the amount of $5 million in punitive damages against the city of Yukon. Following a phone call from a city councilor, Chief Darby ordered Major Angus McDonald to conduct an investigation into the matter as soon as possible. McDonald interviewed neighbors who had witnessed the incident—most from their porches—and concluded by asking them to submit handwritten affidavits regarding what they had observed. These affidavits were then given to Chief Darby, who had still not asked Preston to respond.

By July 29, Chief Darby decided that he had enough documentation to justify disciplinary action against Sgt. Preston; so he asked the city's personnel director, Joe Ulmie, to conduct a disciplinary predetermination (or so-called "Loundermill" hearing) with Preston, as required by ordinance. Ulmie held the hearing and concluded that Preston was indeed guilty of wrongdoing. The following day, Sgt. Preston received a letter in his mailbox at work informing him that he had been given a ten-day suspension without pay and would need to serve the suspension during the first two weeks of August.

## DISCUSSION

1.  If you were an arbitrator reviewing the aforementioned facts, which errors of due process would concern you?

2.  Based on these facts, which arguments would you use to support the following decisions:

    A.  The ten-day suspension should be overturned,

    B.  The ten-day suspension should be modified to a lesser penalty,

    C.  The ten-day suspension should be affirmed.

# 18

## ADA CONCERNS

# Is Heavy Lifting an Essential Job Function?

*The Americans with Disabilities Act of 1990 requires that employers not discriminate against individuals with disabilities. In the employment arena, this means that employers must make "reasonable accommodation" for the disabilities of job applicants and employees who are otherwise qualified.*

Kenneth Jorgenson had been an Automotive Mechanic II with the Equipment Services Department of Maricopa County in Arizona since July 1, 1992. For Jorgenson, the county job meant the end of dead-end jobs as a mechanic that had typified his 25 years of employment. Now, at age 45, Jorgenson could enjoy the security and benefits that came with county employment. When he passed his probationary period in 1993, Ken believed that his financial situation was finally secure, even though Maricopa County had periodically undergone reduction-in-force through employee layoffs.

However, on May 16, 1996, Ken Jorgenson began a slide down the slippery slope to disaster—when he was injured on the job as he lifted a battery out of a box. On June 27, Jorgenson underwent surgery and was hospitalized for eight days; he subsequently returned to work on light duty status on November 11, 1996. For a while, things seemed to be all right, until Jorgenson was reinjured on March 6, 1997. The county moved to terminate Kenneth Jorgenson's employment in April 1997, but held termination in abeyance pending additional medical assessment of Jorgenson's probability for returning to work.

The county justified its intention to terminate him because Jorgenson could no longer perform the essential job duties of an Automotive Mechanic II. Specifically, the job classification specifications for an Automotive Mechanic II included as a requirement the "ability to perform heavy manual labor in the field." An Automotive Mechanic II may be required to lift objects weighing from 50 to 75 pounds. Jorgenson had performed heavy lifting tasks prior to his injury. However, Jorgenson had not met this lifting requirement since May 16, 1996, and was ordered by his physician not to lift anything weighing more than 25 pounds. The county had also given Jorgenson a letter of reprimand on March 6, 1997, for insubordination because he allegedly violated his light duty restrictions. Specifically, Jorgenson was accused of lifting weights of greater than 25 pounds while working in the parts room.

The county's position is that it is not legally prohibited from terminating an employee who is placed on industrial leave status. Kenneth Jorgenson had not performed regular duty as a mechanic for over 13 months, thus placing a tremendous workload burden on other mechanics in the department. The fact that Jorgenson might some day return to work does not compel the county to keep his position open and unfilled by another employee. The needs of the department must take precedence over Jorgenson's desire for a "make work" position. Besides, the county had already assisted Jorgenson, on a humanitarian basis, when it decided not to terminate him until October 1997 in order for him to continue his maximum health care benefits for an additional six months.

Jorgenson's position is that the county acted unfairly by repeatedly trying to terminate his employment since March 1997 for purported reasons that changed several times. Jorgenson contends that he should be maintained on sick leave status, either with or without pay, because he consistently followed county procedures even though these were subsequently revised in an effort to terminate him.

A review of the County's Personnel Procedures #5, "Industrial Leave—Workers' Compensation Benefits Policy and Procedure," sets forth the conditions that must be met before an employee on industrial leave status can be terminated.

1.  The employee ". . . will be off without pay for six months or longer."
2.  The employee's position needs to be filled in order to meet the demands of the management and operational needs of the work unit.
3.  A temporary or on-call person cannot do the job while the employee is off work.
4.  The employee's work cannot be assigned to other workers.
5.  The employee cannot be reassigned to another vacant, less-needed position.
6.  The Risk Management Department has agreed that termination will not seriously threaten the ultimate cost of the industrial case as the appointing authority is ultimately responsible for costs related to industrial cases.
7.  Clearance has been received from the Personnel Department.

Thus, a sequence of events was set into motion by the county's decision to terminate Jorgenson:

• On March 20, 1997, Steve Dugan, Maricopa County manager asked, in writing, for concurrence from Risk Management with his decision to terminate Jorgenson. Hal Hartley, Risk Management department director, replied on March 22, 1997, stating, "I concur that Mr. Jorgenson should be terminated for medical reasons. It is obvious that your department made every effort to provide light duty for him, but the medical information in the industrial file is not enlightening." On April 5, 1997, Lyle Hoffman, bureau chief of the Civil Division of County Legal Services, notified Jorgenson's counsel that Dugan had agreed to postpone any decision of Jorgenson's termination until the results of his MRI were available.

• On April 8, 1997, Dugan again sent a memo to Hartley requesting agreement by Risk Management to terminate

Jorgenson; Dugan stated that the Personnel Department had already consented to the termination. In addressing the aforementioned criteria for termination of an employee while on industrial leave, Dugan made the following points in his memo to Hartley:

1. The workload imposed upon the Automotive Repair division had increased dramatically in the past year and would continue to do so in the future.

2. A temporary or on-call person could not fill the position of Automotive Mechanic II because of the high cost of training and lost productivity. Also, temporary employees can only work up to 90 days and qualified mechanics who are willing to work on a temporary basis are extremely hard to find.

3. The staff level in the division was insufficient to keep up with the workload demand created due to Jorgenson's absence.

4. There were no vacant positions within the department for which Jorgenson was qualified.

On April 10, 1997, Hartley indicated his agreement with Dugan's reasons for seeking Jorgenson's removal. Dugan subsequently decided to delay Jorgenson's termination following a discussion with Lyle Hoffman and Jorgenson's attorney, Frederick Civerollo. Dugan informed Jorgenson on April 23, 1997, that the postponement was based on the fact ". . . that the report from your recent physical examination has not yet been received." Dugan also stated his belief ". . . that the report from the doctor on your condition and the prognosis for your recovery will be instrumental in determining whether to proceed with disciplinary action."

On June 20, 1997, John Roberts, of Risk Management, forwarded the most recent documents regarding Jorgenson's status to Dugan; however, these documents did not indicate whether Jorgenson would ever be able to return to his job with the county. Roberts noted that the county had made repeated efforts to obtain a report from Dr. Perls, Jorgenson's physician, without success. Nonetheless a rehabilitation consultant, Joan Muller, R.N., submitted a report on June 10, 1997, in which she wrote, "His potential for returning to his previous position is unknown. However it would be this consultant's opinion that he most likely will be unable to return to work as a mechanic."

On July 2, 1997, Hartley wrote a memo to Dugan in support of his decision to terminate Jorgenson and reasoned, ". . . you have done everything possible to maintain Jorgenson's employment status prior to his last incident. Your office should be commended for allowing him to work light duty for a considerable length of time. There is no indication when Mr. Jorgenson will return to work, as indeed there may be surgery. . . ." Hartley also encouraged Dugan to give Jorgenson the opportunity to reapply for employment in his department should he ever become fully rehabilitated at some future date.

On July 12, 1997, Jorgenson's attorney, Frederick Civerollo, was advised by Lyle Hoffman, deputy county attorney, that Dugan would consider a request from Jorgenson for medical leave without pay so that he might continue medical insurance benefits for his family. Civerollo formally requested a continuance of medical leave without pay on behalf of Jorgenson on July 16, 1997. Hoffman subsequently admitted on July 24, 1997, that he "was in error to suggest that a request for sick leave without pay was the proper procedure" because Jorgenson's condition was caused by an industrial injury, rather than illness or injury unrelated to the job. However, Hoffman and Dugan proposed an alternate solution: The county would continue to pay medical coverage for Jorgenson through the end of September 1997 and withhold a final decision on his employment status until October 1, 1997. On July 30, 1997, Jorgenson underwent a second back surgery by Dr. Perls.

On September 25, 1997, Civerollo notified Dugan by letter that his client would be unable to return to work as of October 1, 1997, upon the advice of his physician, Dr. Perls. Civerollo requested that the county reconsider its termination decision in light of the fact that Jorgenson was undergoing active medical treatment and therefore receiving temporary total disability benefits. Civerollo again reiterated his request that Jorgenson be allowed to take sick leave without pay. Barbara J. Smythe, a workers compensation employment counselor with GAB Business Services, indicated in a letter to Civerollo that Johnson's first two surgeries involved removal of parts of a vertebral disc.

Smythe stated that Jorgenson would be examined by another neurosurgeon within a couple of weeks in order to obtain a second opinion regarding the possibility of Jorgenson ever going back to work. Smythe also wrote that "it is a *possibility,* not a *probability,* that someone undergoing fusion surgery could ever return to a position that required extensive lifting." Smythe stated that a fusion surgery usually requires up to one year of recovery. Smythe emphasized that Jorgenson already has a permanent disability, but the issue is whether he will ever be able to return to work.

Dugan denied Civerollo's request on September 30, 1997, because ". . . it seems clear that Mr. Jorgenson cannot now, nor in the foreseeable future, perform the duties of Automotive Mechanic II." Dugan also stressed, "It is still imperative that the position assigned to Mr. Jorgenson . . . be filled by an employee able to perform all the duties of the position."

On October 1, 1997, Dugan informed Jorgenson in writing that his employment would be terminated on the effective date of October 4, 1997, because Jorgenson was in violation of the Maricopa County Employee Merit System Resolution, section 17, paragraph C.9, "Inability for Medical Reasons."

Jorgenson was dismissed on the effective date of October 4, 1997, and the stated reason was his violation of the Maricopa County Employee Merit System Resolution, section 17, paragraph C.9, "Inability for Medical Reasons."

## DISCUSSION

1. Discuss the reasons why Maricopa County should (1) terminate Jorgenson, (2) continue their placement attempts elsewhere, or (3) retain Jorgenson on light duty.

2. In your opinion, does the county's termination of Jorgenson violate provisions of the Americans with Disabilities Act?

3. Could Maricopa County have made more "reasonable accommodation" for Jorgenson's disability, and what steps would you recommend?

# 19

## HATCH ACT AND PARTISAN PRACTICES

# Political Shoot-Out in the Lone Star State

*Former Senator Carl Hatch must be turning over in his grave at the way the state of Texas failed to protect the political rights of public employees. These political appointees at the top of these agencies still think that they're working in a campaign in which the number-one ingredient is loyalty to the boss. After all, if you belong to a different political party, you must necessarily be disloyal, and that can't be tolerated.*

Just after Christmas 1997, Ray Barnet, a former employee of the state of Texas, received a large official-looking envelope from the U.S. Department of Labor. "OK, it's just another bureaucratic notification that my appeal has been rejected and I don't need another kick in the face right now," Barnet thought. So Barnet tossed the envelope on the coffee table. When he opened the envelope the next day, Barnet jumped up and down, screaming to his startled wife, "Oh America is beautiful, we've finally been vindicated. Thank God! Hallelujah!" Barnet had just read a civil rights ruling from the U.S. Department of Labor that might bring second thoughts to any state-agency boss who wants to get rid of employees simply because of partisan affiliation.

The Department of Labor ruled that aides to then-Governor Ann Richards, a Democrat, had violated the civil rights of Barnet and seven other mid-level employees of the State Commerce Department by firing them because they were Republicans. The federal agency found that the former employees had been discriminated against and the state of Texas should reinstate them to their former or equivalent jobs, along with back pay plus interest, benefits, and seniority. If carried out, the state could be forced to pay approximately $1.5 million, with each employee eligible for a different amount, based on previous salary and benefits and number of years of employment.

If refused, the state of Texas might lose $439 million in annual federal grants. Barnet thought the state would rather settle with the former workers than risk losing a substantial amount of federal money. Nonetheless, the state quickly made it very clear that the federal decision was not controlling; it announced that it planned to appeal the decision as lacking jurisdiction and being untimely.

## BACKGROUND

The ordeal of the former state employees began in 1990 following the election of Democratic Governor Ann Richards, who immediately appointed two campaign strategists to top posts within the State Commerce Department. These appointees, Ricardo Montoya and Cindy Bonere, wasted no time in announcing their plans to reorganize the department in order to supposedly correct organizational problems that had been detected by federal and state audits. Montoya and Bonere also publicized plans to implement a state version of Vice President Gore's National Performance Review by "reinventing" the State Commerce Department. Accordingly, about 40 employees were targeted for termination through a series of layoffs, including Barnet and his seven coworkers. On April 19, 1991, these eight employees—who also happened to be registered Republicans—received dismissal letters.

Within a few months of losing their jobs, the eight former employees filed complaints with the U.S. Department of Labor, which charged political and age discrimination. They subsequently sued the State Commerce Department in federal district court in two separate actions. In Texas, state employees do not possess a property right to their jobs and serve "at will"; they may be fired for any reason as long as they have not been discriminated against and their civil rights have not been violated. However, state employees do have a constitutional right to belong to the political party of their choice.

The Department of Labor ruling, signed by the civil rights division director, Anna Lockgear, concluded that Montoya had decided to lay off the employees without using a fair assessment process of employee performance. Montoya's criteria for termination were vague and subjective, with the result that a disproportionate number of laid-off employees were registered Republicans, although none held any party posts or had ever run for public office.

Federal juries in each of the two federal trials rejected the laid-off workers' claims of political and age discrimination. Governor Richards testified in both trials; she denied any wrongdoing or partisan agenda. Richards contended that management in the Commerce Department had only been trying to correct administrative problems, reduce inefficiency, and cut spending. After losing the federal trials, the ex-workers appealed their decisions to the U.S. Supreme Court, which failed to consider the matter. Meanwhile, no action was forthcoming from the Department of Labor regarding the complaints by the eight employees.

## THE ORDEAL OF JUSTICE

Anna Lockgear admitted that the Department of Labor's investigation took much too long and that the seven-year wait may be too little, too late for the former employees. Lockgear defended her division's investigation as attributable to limited resources and a case load of nearly 1,300 cases per year. Also, Lockgear underscored the case's uniquenes "'It was our first experience with alleged political discrimination, and we just wanted to make certain that we crossed every 'T' and dotted every 'I' with this investigation."

Unfortunately, the human toll on the dismissed workers was staggering:

• Larry Coughlin, a former budget analyst, suffered severe stress and depression following his dismissal. When he died a few years later, at 62, his widow couldn't afford the funeral expenses and had to take a collection from friends.

• Eddie Aurora, 48, a former maintenance division head, supported his family for two years by mowing lawns, recycling aluminum cans, digging ditches, and painting houses. Aurora told a reporter, "It's way too late, particularly for my friends who really suffered and nearly lost everything. There have been lives and careers destroyed, needlessly." Aurora was finally successful in landing a job as a contract interpreter and translator for the FBI in Dallas.

• Phyllis Simpson, 61, a former budget manager, had to cash in her retirement savings, and she applied for more than a hundred jobs before finding a position with Texas A&M University in Corpus Christi. Upon hearing the news of the Department of Labor ruling, Simpson said, "Only now do I realize how much these unfair firings still hurt."

• Jane Bowen, 66, who later found a position with the Department of Public Safety, told a newspaper reporter, "This was the most devastating thing I've ever had happen to me. It's still very difficult for me to trust anyone because of what they did to us."

• Ray Barnet, 58, suffered a nervous breakdown at the second trial while sitting at the plaintiff's table. Barnet suddenly stood up and started yelling, "I can't take this anymore! I want to go home!" Barnet left sobbing and was taken to Brackenridge Hospital for observation, but he was unable to return to the trial. Barnet still suffers from depression and has not been able to work since April 1991. Barnet's sole support is from disability payments from the Air Force.

• Gene Marcetti, 62, had to collect aluminum cans off the street and lived for a while in a homeless shelter. He was subsequently immobilized by depression.

The remaining former employees felt as if the Department of Labor ruling was vindication for their pain and suffering but viewed it as a bittersweet victory. As Barnet asked, "Why did it take so long? If it had come sooner, we might have avoided two costly trials with accompanying legal fees and avoided the years of emotional damage for many of us." Most of them doubted that they would ever actually receive any back money from the state. A few of the more cynical former employees wondered if perhaps politics had once again reared its ugly head as a reason for the long delay. Could it be that the Clinton administration had forestalled the Department of Labor ruling while Governor Richards was still in office?

## THE STATE REFUSES TO ACQUIESCE

Despite the fact that Texas subsequently elected Republican Governor George W. Bush, state officials seemed little inclined to make peace with the terminated employees. Joe Hilland, general counsel for the Texas Workforce Commission, stated his position, "This amounts to double jeopardy through the back door. These people had their day, make that two days, in court and lost both times. Does anyone really believe that an administrative agency's decision will have precedence over the U.S. Supreme Court?" Hilland also explained that Texas citizens were in no danger of losing money from the federal government because the state would do whatever is necessary to resolve the matter before holding up the money for even one day.

Perhaps the mood of the former employees was most appropriately summed up by Marcetti, who expressed a sense of betrayal by government. "We understand that politicians will always give jobs to fundraisers and campaign workers. That's not what bothers us, because there will be turnover and attrition in state government to create openings. It's when they fire people to put in their friends and cronies that we get upset."

## DISCUSSION

1.  Does the evidence presented support the contention of these former employees that they were dismissed for political reasons?

2.  What other protections against partisanship, if any, should Texas state employees be afforded?

3.   What current options would you propose for resolving this dispute between the state and its former employees?

4.   Is it possible to provide "at will" employment for public employees and still protect their rights to political association?

# III

# HUMAN
# RESOURCES
# MANAGEMENT

# 20

## HUMAN RESOURCES PLANNING

# Smoky Bear
# Is an Underfill

*An "underfill" occurs when an employee who is classified
at a lower grade is moved up to fill a position at a higher
level. One can understand this action if it happens occasionally under management's prerogative of "other duties
as assigned," but there's something awry when an
employee is permanently placed in a higher position with
accompanying duties and responsibilities without the pay
that goes along with that position. That's both bad planning and exploitation by management.*

## BACKGROUND

Right out of high school, Doug Randall began work with the
U.S. Forest Service (USFS) as a firefighter in Chequa-
megon/Nicolet National Forest (CNNF) in Wisconsin in 1980.
Over the next 15 years, Randall received outstanding evaluations and steadily advanced upward, even though the agency
began a reduction-in-force in the 1990s. By 1995, Randall held
the position of Forestry Technician at a GS-7 level and was
assigned to the Dunsmuir Ranger District of the Shasta-Trin-
ity National Forest (STNF) in northern California.

The major responsibilities of the Forestry Technician
position at a GS-7 level are as follows:

1. To plan and manage the recreation sites and activities on the north end of the district.

2. To serve as coordinator on all equal access issues on the district with overall CNNF access responsibilities.

3. To serve as primary supervisor for eight Soil Conservation and Senior Executive Program (SCSEP) employees and one seasonal employee.

4. Operational coordination in planning and budget.

5. Long-range planning and design of recreational facilities.

6. Completion of National Environmental Protection Advocates (NEPA) work related to recreational improvements.

7. To oversee successful operation and maintenance of recreation facilities in the Park Falls area.

8. Supervision of human resource programs as they relate to recreational facilities.

Randall's performance throughout 1995–97 was consistently rated by his supervisors as outstanding. One tongue-in-cheek narrative "gushed over" as follows:

> Many examples of significant achievements: Restoration of campgrounds, trail clearing and step construction, vegetative management, bathroom construction, concrete work . . . all very well done, and certainly a success story. On another note, Doug showed me his latest toilet designs . . . I was flushed with enthusiasm after being in one. His newest has a Lexan clear roof . . . it's like being in a *House and Gardens* atrium . . . light, spacious, friendly, spiritually renewing. Doug is clearly a riser in this subject and is pumped with enthusiasm. Don't raise a big stink about the cost of toilets . . . Doug's much cheaper designs are definitely worth considering. The combination of using senior citizen volunteers, community service crews, home-grown timbers sawn from hazard trees, Lexan clear roofs to view the sky, birds, and the trees along with very attractive and functional modern designs are all contributing to this outstanding step forward in the contemporary toilet movement.

# REORGANIZING THE NATIONAL FOREST

Sometimes the "human side" of human resources planning is lost in the rhetoric of downsizing, reorganization, and reinvention. "Doing more with less" is conveyed as an abstract principle that sometimes is seemingly unconnected to work performed by real people in the field. In June 1994, as part of the USFS initiative to reinvent and redefine its mission, the STNF carried out a series of reorganization moves.

The STNF plan called for the Dunsmuir and Trinity Lake Ranger Districts to be merged into a single district and the workforce downsized by over 30 percent in three years. This was accomplished and, meanwhile, the recreation program grew significantly with visitor-use rates increasing by over 50 percent in many areas. In staffing terms, this translated into reassignment of a majority of recreation work that had previously been accomplished by a Forester (GS-9), Outdoor Recreation Planner (GS-11), and a Forest Landscape Architect (GS-11) to Randall, a GS-7 Forest Technician.

Randall's position description was updated to reflect his reassigned duties. The subsequent job evaluation rated the position at the GS-9 grade. However, this rating did not coincide with the STNF's reorganization plans, which reflected national priorities to "do more with less." The STNF had allocated funds for a Forest Technician at the GS-8 level. Accordingly, Randall agreed to a management compromise—his duties would be reduced to reflect those of a GS-8 rather than the higher duties of a GS-9. Accordingly, Randall was reclassified to a GS-8 grade on August 20, 1995.

Randall notified his supervisor Donna Mackey on August 28 that the following duties should be reduced in their level of expected responsibilities:

• Long-range planning and design of recreational facilities
• Setting of budgetary priorities
• NEPA participation
• Interpretive services

Not only did responsibilities need downgrading, so did performance elements by which Randall's performance would ultimately be evaluated. After all, Randall reasoned, how could management evaluate him against responsibilities that were inaccurately stated?

Randall grew increasingly frustrated as management dragged its feet; no changes were made to his performance elements, nor were any of his position responsibilities ever reduced to the GS-8 level. During the same period, Randall's level of work activity actually increased:

> I have developed community service crews for accomplishment of long-range goals, been involved in the interpretive plan for Trinity Dam, contributed professional input on Forest projects such as Yreka Lake Campground, created new designs of toilets, modified and updated the Forest transition plan, assisted others in fishing pier design, created new cooperative agreements and assumed budget responsibility for community service crews, developed rehabilitation plans for Blue Lake, and been active in the district budgeting process.
>
> None of this should be construed to mean that I'm unhappy with my work situation, my learning opportunities from management, or the like. I'm just requesting that my position description be reexamined, and my grade be established at the proper level.

Finally, human resources specialists in the regional office in San Francisco agreed to conduct another job evaluation of Randall's position, which was completed in March 1997. The result was a recommendation that the Forest Technician position filled by incumbent Randall be reclassified as a GS-9.

Interestingly, the job evaluation report stressed that the primary difference between the work currently performed by Randall and the official GS-8 position description was in Factor 1, "Knowledge Required by the Position." In essence, a GS-9 standard requires the incumbent to exercise "broad recreational responsibilities" with knowledge used to "design, coordinate, and execute complete conventional projects" that are "well-precedented in scientific literature and exercise of judgment based on critical analysis and evaluation of project objectives. . . ." By comparison, a GS-8 standard does not require that "critical analysis and evaluation" be solely performed by the incumbent. Rather, this knowledge resides in the incumbent's supervisor, who is graded at a higher level. However, the job evaluation confirmed that Randall had regularly utilized broad discretion in performing the duties of a Forest Technician during the 1994–97 period.

Clearly management had two options; either it could (1) remove the work from the position performed by Randall, or (2) it could noncompetitively promote Randall to a GS-9 level and presumably pay him at the GS-9 level for the last three years. With the former option, one can reasonably question whether it would be fair or appropriate to remove work, considering that those duties have been performed for several years.

Finally on April 29, 1997, Robert Heinny, district ranger, informed Randall by memo that management had made its decision regarding his requested upgrade: Randall would be retained in his current GS-8 Forestry Technician position and Randall's supervisor must perform the GS-9 work identified in the desk audit. Heinny reasoned, "This will place us in line with the long-term organization plan." Heinny also noted, "We plan to recognize you for your extra effort this past year." Off the record, Heinny let it be known that promoting Randall could "cause resentment from other employees." Randall was dumbfounded: "How does one take back knowledge that I already have in my head?" Furthermore, where's the logic of asking Randall's supervisor, who was already overworked, to perform additional duties that Randall had quite capably performed for three years? It seemed to Randall that management was not going to recognize his work at the GS-9 level because it simply wasn't in the reorganization plan and therefore couldn't be allowed.

## DISCUSSION

1.  How can human resources planning prevent long-term underfills from occurring?

2.  Is it really possible to "do more with less" when it comes to reorganizing?

3.  How would you recommend that Randall and the district ranger resolve their dispute regarding Randall's job duties?

# 21

## PERFORMANCE EVALUATION

# To Protect and
# to Serve

*The motto of the Los Angeles Police Department is "to pro-tect and to serve." How are Angelenos being "served" by the chief of police forcing his police officers to write a set number of traffic tickets each month? All that's going to do is make the public even madder at the department, and that's not a smart thing to do in the aftermath of the Rodney King incident, the recent race riots in South Central Los Angeles, and the racist revelations of Mark Fuhrman during the O.J. Simpson trial.*

Tensions between a white mayor and a black police chief (or vice versa) are nothing new in the city of Los Angeles; there is a long history going all the way back to the 1960s with the bitter in-fighting between Mayor Sam Yorty and Chief Tom Bradley. It was later continued between Chief Daryl Gates and Mayor Bradley. It also spills over in conflict between the chief and the union, the Los Angeles Police Protective League (LAPPL), which now finds itself embroiled in a debate regarding how police officer productivity should be measured.

Police Chief Bernard C. Parks, who was the first black chief since Bradley and a positive contrast to his predecessor, Gates, was known as a no-nonsense administrator. Chief Parks did little to endear himself to the troops in 1997 when he unilaterally eliminated the three-day work week that was widely supported but which Parks argued had the effect of reducing services to the community.

Further deterioration occurred when Chief Parks restructured the grievance process and proposed changes in the city charter that would have strengthened his own decision-making authority. The most recent flash point happened in 1998, when Chief Parks announced a renewed departmental focus on individual officer accountability as the key component of his community policing program. Performance evaluation criteria would be developed in each of the Los Angeles Police Department's (LAPD) divisions by which officer performance could be quantitatively compared against all other officers in the same division. Predictably, LAPPL President Garth Moran criticized the chief's approach as a numbers game that was not in the best interests of the community.

Moran was particularly incensed with a performance productivity plan devised by Capt. Bobby Hanson, who had recently been put in command of LAPD's Harbor Division. Moran criticized Hanson for allegedly improperly comparing officers along the following 12 categories:

• issuance of traffic and parking citations
• conducting field interviews
• quality of incident reports
• correctly responding to radio communications
• following arrest procedures
• safety skills
• maintenance of equipment
• reliability
• judgment and common sense
• attendance
• performance improvement log entries

Moran attacked the chief's performance evaluation program as "smoke and mirrors" to hide the fact that quotas were being mandated from the top. Key LAPD officials vehemently denied that the performance evaluation criteria caused the creation of quotas. They maintained that the criteria simply helped supervisors determine whether officers are doing their jobs or being productive.

In an effort to promote more light than heat on the subject, Chief Parks asked his chief-of-staff, Commander Don Kalishman, to meet with Moran and see if greater understanding could be attained regarding the chief's new productivity focus. Garth Moran (GM) agreed to meet with Don Kalishman (DK), and the following excerpts were taken from their off-the-record conversation at the San Fernando Valley Division Headquarters:

**GM:** Don, the captains in LAPD are running scared because the chief is breathing down their necks about this new productivity thing. They're afraid of being criticized, so they all want their numbers to be up. You know, give us more citations and arrests. These are "quotas" and this isn't in anyone's best interest.

**DK:** Look Garth, I don't believe in quotas, it's merely a way of measuring officer performance. It's done all the time in corporate America.

**GM:** Are you kidding me? Measuring individual officer performance is not where it's at anymore; employee performance evaluations have gone the way of the dinosaur. The new cutting-edge techniques, such as total quality management (TQM), put the evaluation emphasis on teams and group incentives. Your system encourages officers to compete against one another rather than working as a team.

**DK:** Productivity statistics were not intended to be the sole measurement of an officer's job productivity, but they certainly are a key indicator of what officers are doing out in the field. It's not the numbers that matter, the chief wants us to focus on the end result. Are we "mission driven" and "results oriented"? There was one officer who came up with some good suggestions for building a better working relationship between the North Hollywood Hispanic community and the department. That's the kind of result that the chief wants to encourage.

**GM:** There you go again with that bull-shit jargon that doesn't mean anything to the rank-and-file officers.

We're supposed to be doing "community policing" in L.A.
but no one knows what that means either. Under community policing the officer should get to know his community or barrio so that citizens are involved in fighting
crime. This requires time for the officers to stop and talk
to neighbors while they're out on patrol. So where does
this philosophy fit into the chief's focus on productivity?
If you take the time to get to know the community, your
numbers will be down. So what in the hell does the chief
want—to churn out the arrests and citations or slow
down and get to know people in the communities?

**DK:** You know, Garth, the only officers who have complained about the chief's productivity emphasis are the
ones who are unproductive. I believe in making certain
that the officers who work for me really work hard and
aren't just killing time in a donut shop getting to know
the neighborhood. We understand that occasionally
even the best officer will have an off day but, come on,
we've got to have minimum standards and criteria over
a period of time by which to find out who the loafers
are in this department.

**GM:** I really resent your comments about my fellow officers. They're out there busting their buns on the
streets while you and your M.B.A. types in the Parker
Center concoct some new performance evaluation
scheme that isn't even state of the art. For example,
hasn't it always been left to officer discretion to decide
whether to issue a citation or not? This new system
forces us to inflate those numbers whenever possible.
And whatever happened to teamwork? This new system will result in several officers at a crime scene, each
trying to take credit as the arresting officer. Everyone
will want to "hot dog" it to get those numbers way up.

**DK:** I'm not trying to put anybody down and, by the way,
I've put my time in out in the field just like everyone
else. I started out as a detective in the violent crimes
division; later on I became a captain of the patrol division and commanding officer of criminal investigations
I'll have you know that, for what it's worth, I didn't get
an M.B.A.; I've got an M.P.A. from Cal State,
Dominguez Hills. I'm certainly aware of TQM and the

quality movement, but frankly, all that "continuous quality improvement" stuff and "self-directed work teams" business just doesn't cut it in police work, particularly in a city like Los Angeles. Our philosophy is that even though an officer in the field depends on support and backup from fellow officers in case of emergency or during an investigation, police work is still basically handled by individual officers. It isn't a team that decides to give a citation to a speeding motorist or initiate a chase on foot; it's the beat cop, and that's the type of work that can be easily documented for productivity.

**GM:** Sorry, I wasn't putting down your degree. In fact, I'm getting a B.A. in Criminal Justice from Cal State, Fullerton. But it seems to most of us in the union that you guys have forgotten your roots and what really works out here in the field. It's just that the chief's quantitative rating system sets an illegal quota that punishes officers who fail to reach arbitrary goals in ticket writing and other police duties. It isn't fair to the officers or the citizens of Los Angeles. Officers should be judged by their overall performance in the field, as witnessed and documented by front-line supervisors.

**DK:** Well, frankly we've tried that approach and it doesn't work very well. We let sergeants set individual objectives for each officer and these usually turned out to be unrealistically low because no one wanted to crack the whip. So we went back to a system that relied on hard data and compared officers' performances to one another.

Well, I see that it's about time to end things for today. Maybe we can meet again next Monday if you want?

**GM:** That would be fine with me. Oh, by the way, we're getting a little bit pissed off with allowing captains and lieutenants, who aren't even these officers' supervisors, to change evaluation ratings given out by sergeants. These people don't know the officers, but they've got in mind some set percentages of how many officers should fall into certain rating categories. It's unfair and illegal to evaluate someone you don't even know. Maybe that's an issue we could discuss in the future.

# DISCUSSION

1. Discuss the advantages and disadvantages of the chief's new performance productivity plan.

2. What are the prospects for TQM and team approaches to performance evaluation in paramilitary agencies?

3. What recommendations would you make for implementing a performance evaluation system at the LAPD?

# 22

## EMPLOYEE DEVELOPMENT AND TRAINING

# Fearless Freddy Fuego

*Lake Havasu City, Arizona, has been the butt of countless jokes because of the London Bridge, which was reconstructed across to an island in the lake. The most exciting event in this mostly sleepy retirement community has nothing to do with the London Bridge; it occurs every spring break, when thousands of college kids from Arizona ("zonies") and California converge in their boats to Copper Cove. For an entire week, the mass of boats forms a solid floor for dancing, drinking, and just general partying. It's the one time of the year when Lake Havasu's small paramedic force stays very busy!*

Freddy Fuego had been, up until the time of his sudden demotion from fire captain, a full-time, classified employee of Lake Havasu City since August 24, 1981, and seemed to have a promising career ahead of him with the fire department as a paramedic supervisor. However, his career prospects were seriously dampened when Fuego was demoted from fire captain, salary range 40, to fire engineer, salary range 30, on the effective date of April 23, 1998. Fuego's career took a nosedive because he did not maintain sufficient continuing education hours to be certified as a paramedic and was demoted for failing to do so. The story of how a seemingly foolish challenge to management's authority could cost a career can be attributed to Fuego's determination to go head to head with the fire chief over what Fuego considered to be an excessive and unnecessary training requirement.

In order to maintain their certification, paramedics in Arizona are required by the state to attend 12 hours of "tape and chart" sessions each year. These meetings are conducted by medical personnel at designated "base hospitals" throughout the state, of which Havasu Samaritan Regional Hospital (HSRH) is the regional hospital serving the Lake Havasu City Fire Department (LHCFD). Gerald Grant, M.D., serves as the medical review officer at HSRH and in that capacity reviews the performance of LHCFD paramedics; he also sets continuing education requirements for paramedics covered by his "medical control." Dr. Grant and HSRH have mandated that paramedics under their medical jurisdiction attend 12 meetings, each lasting two hours, although paramedics may be excused from attending three sessions if necessary. Thus, LHCFD paramedics must attend a minimum of 18 hours; whereas the state's required minimum is only 12 hours. Paramedics who fail to attend the required tape and chart sessions lose their medical control and are not authorized to practice as paramedics in Mojave County, where the LHFCD is located.

Fuego had long been bothered by the additional continuing education requirements imposed by Mojave County in comparison to other jurisdictions in Arizona. Fuego asserted that his primary job duties and responsibilities are as a firefighter rather than a paramedic; he should not be in trouble for allowing his "medical control" certification to lapse because of an arbitrary decision by medical personnel at the base hospital. Furthermore, Fuego had complied with the basic state continuing education requirement of 12 hours even though the base hospital in Lake Havasu mandated 18 hours for all paramedics in Mojave County. Because base hospital medical personnel were not in his chain of command, Fuego believed he should not be compelled to follow their guidelines for an additional six hours of continuing certification. So, Fuego decided to wage a one-person protest against these additional requirements.

Problems began when Fuego attended a January 16, 1998, tape and chart meeting in which it was announced that the March 31, 1998, deadline for completing continuing education requirements would be enforced. On February 18, Battalion Chief Jack Jacobi delivered a notice to Fuego from HSRH that Fuego was lacking two sessions, which must be completed before April 1 or medical control privileges would be suspended. Fuego indicated to Jacobi that he would take care of the problem. On February 27, Fuego turned back the memo with a notation that tape and chart meetings were scheduled for March 6 and 9, 1998, and he planned to attend. However, Fuego did not show up for either of those meetings.

Things came to a head on Wednesday, April 1, 1998, when Fuego was relieved from duty at 7:05 A.M. by Jacobi because Fuego's medical control as a paramedic had been removed; he was placed on administrative leave with pay. Jacobi informed Fuego that he must see Chief Frederick on Monday, April 3. Fuego informed Jacobi that he already had a prior commitment on April 3 to take a friend back to Phoenix. Jacobi emphasized the urgency of meeting with Chief Frederick on Friday. Deputy Chief Doug Clevenger had a telephone conversation with Fuego during the evening of April 3, during which Fuego informed Clevenger that he still had not completed his continuing education requirements and therefore had not been cleared to work as a paramedic. Fuego indicated to Clevenger that it was time someone challenged the unfair burden imposed by the number of tape and chart meetings mandated by HSRH and that he was in the best position to do so. Why should paramedics in Lake Havasu, simply because they were located in Mojave County, be compelled to attend extra classes that were not required of paramedics in Flagstaff or Prescott?

Fuego intended to make his point and meet with Chief Frederick in order to resolve the issue. On Friday, April 3, Fuego attempted to telephone Chief Frederick several times without success; he then went to Phoenix and returned at the end of the shift but was unable to meet with Chief Frederick. On the following Monday morning, April 6, the newly nicknamed "Fearless Freddy" met with Chief Frederick in his office regarding his status. Following the meeting, a greatly subdued Fuego agreed to comply with the county's continuing education requirement; his medical control was reestablished on April 7, 1998. The chief and Fuego met again on April 20 in an administrative review meeting in which Fuego again explained his actions and position in some detail, while the chief politely listened and then reiterated the need to comply with training certification or face disciplinary action.

Finally, exasperated with Fuego's passive resistance, the chief sent a notice of intent to discipline to Fuego and apprised him of a predetermination hearing set in the chief's office on April 22. The chief's letter described the charges and factual basis for proposed disciplinary action. Specifically, Fuego was charged with violating the following rules as contained in the city's *Personnel Rules and Regulations:*

- *Rule 4. Section 405.C.1:* "The employee lacks sufficient competency or efficiency to perform assigned duties and responsibilities. . . ."
- *Rule 4. Section 405.C.4:* "The employee has . . . failed to follow reasonable direction from a supervisor. . . ."

---

Fuego was notified of the following grounds for his demotion: "Your medical control privileges were suspended by the Base Hospital medical director, leaving you unable to perform any medical functions at an emergency scene. This was preceded by repeated warnings, both verbal and written, detailing what was required to keep your medical privileges. You also did not give the Fire Department any notice that you were not going to comply with the Base Hospital requirements, which left us without your services as the captain of your crew for the shift of April 1, 1998. You further refused to resolve the problem, which made you unavailable for your shift of April 6, 1998." Chief Frederick went on to explain, "This is, without a doubt, a level of service that I cannot tolerate from a fire captain, and certainly does not follow the Management by Example/Fact process under which we work."

At his predetermination (often referred to as "Loudermill" because of the landmark U.S. Supreme Court decision in 1985) hearing on April 22, Fuego urged Chief Frederick to take into consideration that he had been a dedicated employee with an outstanding work record for over 17 years. The chief informed Fuego that he intended to give him a demotion, unless there were mitigating factors that Fuego could produce. Fuego's position was that perhaps he deserved an oral reprimand for his actions, but the city would not be able to demonstrate through a preponderance of evidence admitted at a hearing that the demotion was positive and corrective in nature; even if he was legally guilty of wrongdoing, a demotion was overly severe as a disciplinary penalty. Fuego also was upset because he believed he had been more severely disciplined by demotion than other employees who had let their medical control lapse over the years. Fuego felt that he was being made an example because of his supervisory status.

The fire chief's position was that Fuego held a management position as fire captain and was expected to set an example for other employees. By his refusal to maintain job qualifications and willingly ignoring directives to maintain his paramedic certification, he represents an unacceptable role model for a fire captain. The chief contended that Fuego deliberately and openly challenged LHCFD policies and did not independently comply with certification requirements when he was initially placed on administrative suspension. The city's imposition of a demotion rather than a less severe disciplinary penalty stemmed from his higher rank and Fuego's failure to immediately seek medical control reinstatement.

Following the hearing, the chief asked city attorney Sue Alire to conduct a review of the city's personnel records for possible disparate treatment. These records subsequently revealed that several other LHCFD employees had been disciplined when their medical control privileges lapsed; they received either a shift suspension or letter of reprimand. Fuego was the first LHCFD supervisor to be demoted because of the aforementioned infraction. In all other instances, employees missed only one shift and completed the continuing education hours prior to the start of the next scheduled shift.

The city attorney reviewed the events surrounding Fuego's proposed demotion and offered her opinion that the city was prepared to shoulder the burden of proof to demonstrate in a grievance hearing, through the preponderance of evidence, just cause to discipline Fuego for wrongdoing. The city attorney argued that Fuego knew and understood the continuing education requirements for paramedics covered by HSRH. These rules had been in effect over a long period of time and were consistently applied. It was also well known to Fuego that HSRH required more hours than many other base hospitals throughout Arizona and more than the state-mandated minimum amount. Moreover, it was incontestable that a base hospital has delegated autonomy to require any reasonable number of hours that it deems appropriate for all paramedics or particular individual paramedics under its medical control.

The city attorney refuted Fuego's argument that he was not compelled to follow directives from HSRH staff because they are not members of Fuego's chain of command or even Lake Havasu City employees. The city attorney argued that the LHCFD does not set medical standards for its paramedics; medical standards are set by medical doctors. Fuego has not been given discretion to decide the extent or the content of continuing education units. The city attorney contended that paramedics practice under the umbrella authorization of a licensed physician with appropriate specialization, and Lake Havasu is contractually obligated to comply with continuing education standards set by HSRH.

Alire also offered several aggravating factors in support of management's decision to demote Fuego from the rank of fire captain. First, it is an accepted principle that an employee who believes a lawful rule is unfair is to obey the rule and protest later. No employee can rightfully disobey clear and unambiguous rules at will. It is the employee's obligation to protest or appeal a rule through authorized channels. Secondly, an employee who holds a management position is held to a higher standard of performance and behavior. As a fire captain, Fuego supervised paramedic employees and was a role model for all employees; he does not have the liberty to openly disregard agency rules. Fuego was repeatedly warned that rules would be enforced by a stated deadline, and he promised to comply. Not only did Fuego fail to carry out a management policy on April 1, he again did nothing to correct the deficiency until faced with a possible discharge. As a manager, Fuego should be reasonably expected to openly support all policies and procedures in an exemplary manner.

The fire chief received the city attorney's analysis and recommendations and proceeded to carry out the demotion of Fearless Freddy Fuego.

## DISCUSSION

1. You are a close friend and coworker of Fuego; what advice would you give him regarding whether to appeal the demotion?

2. You are the fire chief, and Deputy Chief Clevenger has come to you asking you not to impose the demotion and to give Fuego one more opportunity to obtain certification as a paramedic in Mojave County. How would you respond to Clevenger?

3. You are the fire chief and you have been approached by the human resources director and asked to consider a mediation with Fuego by an outside mediator. Would you be open to mediation, even with a subordinate employee?

# 23

# Eenie-Meenie-
# Miny-Mo

*"Eenie-meenie-miny-mo" is a rather cute and time-honored way among children to select who will be assigned to a task that no one else wishes to perform. While charming when used by children, it is much more serious when applied by decision makers to decide which employees will lose their jobs.*

The human stories behind landmark U.S. Supreme Court cases are often full of all the emotion and conflict that one can imagine. Consider the real events and individuals involved in the U.S. Supreme Court's "almost decision" in *Piscataway Board of Education v. Taxman.* On one side was Debra Williams, an African American high school business teacher, who became a reluctant symbol of affirmative action when the Piscataway, New Jersey, school board, pressed to lay off one of ten teachers in its high school business department, kept Williams while dismissing a white teacher, who was deemed equally qualified. The white teacher, Sharon Taxman, hired by the same department on the same day as Williams, was laid off because of the school district's affirmative action policy that expressed preference for retaining members of groups protected by affirmative action if all other qualifications are equal (of course, being women, both Williams and Taxman were covered by the district's affirmative action plan). The board decided to keep Debra Williams to promote diversity for its students—30 percent of whom are African American.

Following her layoff, Taxman decided to fight back against what she considered to be an unfair policy directed against whites simply because of their race; she filed a discrimination complaint that ultimately reached the U.S. Supreme Court. Taxman ultimately got her job back in 1992, but she continued her pursuit of back pay. A federal judge ruled in her favor in 1993 and awarded her $144,000, which was appealed to the U.S. Court of Appeals for the Third Circuit. Taxman alleged that the board's affirmative action plan violated Title VII of the Civil Rights Act of 1964 by condoning "reverse discrimination." The court subsequently ruled that, under Title VII, employers could never use diversity as a reason for making employment decisions based on race. Only race-related measures that were aimed at remedying current or lingering discrimination were permitted under Title VII, the appeals court ruled. In essence, the board's decision to lay off Taxman in order to achieve greater diversity had "unnecessarily trammeled her interests."

The appellate court decision was ultimately appealed to the U.S. Supreme Court where it appeared to be destined by many observers to become the most significant Court decision regarding affirmative action since the historic *Bakke* ruling in 1978. However, in an unexpected move that was aimed to avert what could have been a fatal blow to affirmative action, the Black Leadership Forum raised 70 percent of the money necessary to fund an out-of-court settlement by the school district of $433,500 with Taxman to prevent the Piscataway case from reaching the high court. Thus, the legal battle between Taxman and the Piscataway board seemed to be over; but the racial scars generated by this case are deep and may not heal for many years to come, if ever.

Consider the following psychological effects in 1997 of the long court struggle on the principal participants, Taxman (age 50) and Williams (age 45), who, even though they share adjoining offices, rarely speak to each other:

- *Sharon Taxman* was described as having dealt with the ordeal of the eight-and-one-half-year-old court case by reportedly withdrawing from colleagues and extracurricular activities and allegedly refusing to discuss her case with anyone but family and her lawyer—who described the case's impact on Taxman as "depressing." When Taxman's lawyer was apprised that Williams was angry over the prolonged legal battle, he responded that Williams had nothing to be upset about: "She didn't miss any paychecks" (September 29, 1997).

- *Debra Williams*, on the other hand, threw herself into graduate school with a full course load and volunteerism, thus waging a crusade to prove she wasn't kept as a teacher just because she was African American. Williams was quoted as saying, "I would rather think that they kept me because I was qualified. I don't want other black kids, Asians and Hispanics . . . to read in the paper that they only kept Ms. Williams because she was another lonely black teacher needing a job" (November 22, 1997). Also upsetting to Williams, who was at the school board meeting and sobbed after the settlement was reached, was the fact that she considered herself far more qualified than Taxman because she has a master's degree and Taxman doesn't. Williams finished a master's degree in business education shortly after arriving at Piscataway, while Taxman never completed her graduate degree (but Taxman came to the school with three years' experience teaching business, while Williams had less than one). Williams commented after the meeting, "You don't get nothing in this world for having an advanced degree; you get nothing but a slap in the face" (November 22, 1997). As the legal battle has dragged on, Williams said that her blood pressure has risen sharply and the case has strained relations with her supervisors.

Finally, it is interesting to note that under terms of the settlement, Taxman will get $186,000 (out of $433,500) in back pay and interest. Her attorneys will get the remainder.

# DISCUSSION

1. What are the lessons and "missed opportunities" that can be gleaned from the efforts of the Piscataway School Board to follow its affirmative action plan and increase workplace diversity?

2. Assume that you have just been appointed principal of the Piscataway Township High School. What actions would you take to reduce conflict and improve morale in the Business Education Department as well as throughout the school?

3. In retrospect, how would you think that the school board should have approached the issue of layoff in 1989?

Quotes taken from: "Racial Case Scars Two NJ Teachers," *Albuquerque Journal*, September 29, 1997, A-7; "Racial-Preference Suit Settled," *Albuquerque Journal*, November 22, 1997, A-10.

# 24

## DISPARATE TREATMENT IN DISCIPLINARY ACTION

# Cattery Row

*cattery—noun, pl. -teries (circa 1834): an establishment for the breeding and boarding of cats. (Webster's Ninth New Collegiate Dictionary, 1983. Merriam-Webster, Inc., Publishers, Springfield, Mass.)*

Elisa Baca had been employed at the city of Albuquerque's Animal Control Center (ACC) immediately out of Rio Grande High School five years ago and things had gone fairly smoothly until about six months earlier. Baca had hoped that a full-time job at ACC, hardly a glamour position with the city, would be her ticket out of the tough gang territory of Albuquerque's south valley. Everything was fine at work until Magdalena "Maggie" Romero was assigned to the ACC; this was bad news because Romero and Baca had a torrid relationship about two years ago, which ended when Baca became afraid of Romero's mood swings and sometimes violent behavior. But Romero was not one to let sleeping dogs lie. Finally, Baca moved to another apartment and had put in a private line in hopes of severing the relationship with Romero, who worked as a correctional officer at the Bernalillo County Detention Center.

Baca's calm was shattered when she heard the news that Romero had obtained a transfer from the jail to the ACC, obviously to be near Baca. Since ending the relationship with Romero, Baca had become good friends with Annette Lujan, who also worked at the ACC (although they were not romantically involved and Lujan was actually straight). It wasn't long before Romero had singled out Lujan as someone to particularly torment. On one particular lunch break at a nearby café, Romero walked up to the table where Lujan and Baca were eating lunch. Romero pretended to inadvertently spill her Diet Coke on Lujan, who immediately pushed Romero. Romero shoved her back as they yelled at each other. Baca's supervisor and veterinarian at the ACC, Dr. Jane Owen, quickly broke up the altercation. As a consequence, both Romero and Lujan received a disciplinary action of five days' leave without pay. As Dr. Owen explained, she wrote them up for "scuffling" rather than "fighting," because fighting would have resulted in automatic dismissal under city policies. However, Dr. Owen warned that any repeated offense would most surely result in summary discharge!

Approximately six months later, Romero was assigned to work the Kennels during day shift on an exceptionally hot day, even for Albuquerque. As the shift wore on and the thunderclouds began to build up over the Sandia Mountains, Romero became increasingly irritable. The female Great Dane in the third cage–south didn't help Romero's temperament by growling and baring her teeth every time Romero walked by. Finally, Romero decided she'd had enough and would take matters into her own hands. Romero left the Kennels area and walked quickly over the 50 yards to the Cattery building, where Baca was working.

The Cattery, a dimly lit room barely 12 x 14 feet, had a low ceiling with wire cages from floor to ceiling on each of its four walls. As usual, the cages were filled to capacity with unwanted or lost cats. Baca was at her desk at the far end of the room from the door when Romero entered. Standing in the doorway, Romero with a hand on her hip, looked at Baca and sneeringly said in Spanish a phrase that meant that Baca's mother had not been legally married at the time of Baca's birth. Shaking, Baca asked Romero to repeat what she had just said. Romero took several steps forward until she was just inches in front of Baca and uttered another profanity in Spanish. Baca erupted and caught Romero with a left hook to her mouth, causing Romero to bleed profusely.

Romero grabbed Baca around the neck, and both women fell to the floor as they continued to punch, scratch, and pull each other's hair.

Agitated by all the commotion, the cats in the cages started to screech and howl. As the women struggled, the cat cages were kicked and several fell to the floor, even further exciting the feline occupants. While passing by the Cattery, Owen heard loud noises and the high-pitched screeches of upset cats. Owen rushed in, observed the ensuing fight, and in her best command voice, ordered Baca and Romero to cease immediately. Owens also instructed Romero to leave the Cattery; however, Romero refused to move and Owen then walked Baca to the ACC headquarters.

Both Baca and Romero were immediately discharged for fighting. Each, in separate grievance hearings, appealed her disciplinary actions.

## DISCUSSION

1.  A city hearing officer subsequently conducted grievance appeal hearings for Elisa Baca and Maggie Romero. If you had been the hearing officer, what recommendation would you make? Keep in mind that you have one of the following three choices: (1) uphold the termination, (2) reverse the termination and thereby reinstate the employee, or (3) modify the termination to a lesser disciplinary action and reinstate the employee.

2.  In actuality, the hearing officer recommended that one of the discharged employees be given a 90-day suspension without pay and reinstated to her former position with the city; the discharge of the other employee was upheld. The hearing officer cited three mitigating circumstances in his decision to modify the termination. Decide:

    •  Which employee did the hearing officer reinstate?

    •  What were the three likely factors influencing his decision to reinstate?

# 25

## PREPONDERANCE OF EVIDENCE
## IN DISCIPLINE

# The Case of the Missing
# Portable Potty

*Usually, an employer who disciplines an employee in a
government agency must defend the action in a grievance
hearing. One of the key decisions that an employer makes
is whether to discharge the employee outright or apply the
principle of "progressive discipline," for which there is no
precise definition or formula. An employer who chooses
the former must always be prepared to show through the
the preponderance of evidence that the infraction was so
serious that progressive discipline would not have corrected the employee's egregious behavior. This is particularly true in matters where a worker has been charged
with acts of moral turpitude—theft, embezzlement, drug
use, or immorality.*

On December 22, 1997, Thomas Montana, who was assistant
finance director of the county of Santa Fe, New Mexico, conducted a review of invoices received from various vendors as
a part of his normal work duties. Montana didn't notice anything unusual during his review, until he came across certain
invoices received from J & J Portable Toilets, Inc. The first
invoice was for a portable toilet that had been delivered to an
address on Kathryn Street. This fact struck Montana as

peculiar in that this address is located within the city limits of Santa Fe. Because Montana did not believe the county would order a portable toilet for delivery within the city, Montana telephoned J & J to determine if the invoices erroneously had been sent to the county. Montana was informed by J & J that, according to their records, the portable toilet had been ordered by Orlando Guerra in the Land Use Department and was to be delivered to 627 Kathryn Street. Upon reviewing Guerra's personnel file, it was determined that Guerra's home address was listed as 627 Kathryn Street. Montana was puzzled; why would a county employee order a portable potty sent to a home address at county expense?

Montana contacted Carlos Onadia, Guerra's supervisor, on January 9, 1998, to inform him of what he had discovered. Together, Onadia and Montana telephoned J & J and spoke with Rita Olmas, an employee who indicated that she had taken the order for a portable toilet via telephone on October 16, 1997, from someone who identified himself as Orlando Guerra. Olmas also stated that the caller asked her to deliver the toilet to 627 Kathryn Street and that the toilet rental should be charged to the county of Santa Fe, under the same purchase order number as assigned to the "Jacona order."

Montana continued his investigation and also discovered a second invoice. Coincidentally, Tom Bender, an employee with the Public Works Department, had placed an order with J & J on October 16, 1997, for a portable toilet to be delivered to County Road 84 in Jacona. When Montana called Bender, he was informed that Bender was only aware of his own order for a portable toilet and that he and Guerra were not personally acquainted. Montana also realized that the Public Works Department and Land Use Department were not physically located in close proximity to each other. Thus, there seemed to be no obvious way that Guerra could have had access to the Bender order for work in Jacona.

Later the same day, Onadia and Karla Quinn, who was personnel director for the county, met with Guerra and apprised him of the information that they had received from J & J, although they did not relay Bender's comments to Guerra. Onadia and Quinn also informed Guerra that he would be placed on administrative leave with pay pending further investigation of the matter and that he faced possible termination, depending on the outcome of the investigation. When confronted by Onadia and Quinn, Guerra admitted that on October 19, 1997, he had been remodeling his house. At some point during the remodeling work Guerra said that he and his wife determined that the entire bathroom would need to be replaced, instead of the planned minor repairs to the existing bathroom. As a convenience to the workers and to protect the family's privacy in their home, Guerra decided to rent a portable toilet from J & J. Guerra placed the order by telephone and the toilet was delivered the same day. Guerra denied that he gave the J & J order taker, who was unknown to him at that time, a county purchase order number or ever indicated that the toilet should be billed to the County Road Department.

Following the meeting with Onadia and Quinn, Guerra later telephoned J & J and spoke with Olmas, who, when confronted by Guerra, denied that she had inadvertently made a mistake with the purchase order. Upset because he had been placed on administrative leave and faced with Olmas's steadfast denial of wrongdoing, Guerra visited J & J and asked that Olmas prepare a written statement in which she would admit making a mistake on Guerra's purchase order number and order form; Olmas refuse to comply with Guerra's request. Guerra paid his bill of approximately $200 for the portable toilet and slammed the door behind him.

## THE INVESTIGATION

Quinn was assigned the task of conducting the fact-finding investigation and submitting a report containing recommendations to the county manager within two weeks. A review by Quinn of Guerra's personnel file produced the following information:

• Guerra was employed by Santa Fe County from April 6, 1993, through the date of his discharge in the Land Use Department. Guerra was initially hired as a Code Enforcement Inspector, and he subsequently was transferred to the position of Plats Examiner. On July 22, 1995, Guerra was promoted, upon the recommendation of his supervisor, Onadia, to the position of Development Review Specialist I. Guerra received a rating of "satisfactory" on his only Performance Planning and Evaluation Form, which was given on April 15, 1996.

• The order form prepared by Olmas on October 19, based on her alleged conversation with Guerra, records two telephone numbers as follows: 555-6228 (written directly above the line for "Phone #") and 555-6332 (written above the first telephone number in slightly smaller numbers). The 555-6228 number was verified as Guerra's work number in Land Use; the second number was a number in Public Works and was also the only telephone number listed on the purchase order by Bender on October 16. Both order forms indicate the same purchase order (P.O.) number of 053672.

• Guerra was an active member of a local of the American Federation of State, County, and Municipal Employees (AFSCME), which had recently organized Santa Fe County employees. Specifically, Guerra served as a union observer during the certification election just prior to his discharge, although no one had conclusive evidence to corroborate Guerra's theory that his union activities were considered by management in its decision to place him on administrative leave.

• Quinn reviewed the Olmas affidavit; it centered on Olmas's recollection on January 12, 1998, of what she remembered regarding a routine order prepared on October 19, 1997, one of perhaps 20 to 30 that she prepared that same day. Quinn reasoned that it was not inconceivable that Olmas simply made a mistake by confusing a county phone number from an order that she had received just three days earlier; it was plausible to assume that a reasonable person using common sense had made a mistake.

Quinn then proceeded to examine the county's security policies and procedures for purchasing and financial record keeping. What she found would not be supportive of strong disciplinary action against Guerra:

• Authorized county personnel are required to undertake certain security measures regarding the assignment and disposition of P.O. numbers.

• First, only designated employees in each department were permitted to obtain P.O. numbers, and Guerra was not so authorized.

• Second, requests for P.O. numbers by unauthorized individuals would need to be verified by contacting an authorized employee.

• Third, only Mariana Toyo, an administrative assistant in Land Use at the time of the incident, was authorized to contact Finance in order to obtain a P.O. number.

• Fourth, P.O. forms were not readily available or unlocked during office hours.

• Authorized county personnel must comply with designated security procedures in order to gain access through the computer to P.O. numbers. Authorized employees must obtain a password from the Management Information Systems Department, following approval by the Land Use director. Passwords must be changed every 30 to 60 days; there was no indication that Guerra ever received a password.

The evidence against Guerra is completely circumstantial in a matter wherein his honesty and reputation in the community are at stake.

Quinn could not unravel the "mystery" regarding how Guerra could have obtained the previous P.O. number from a Public Works document. This puzzle was compounded by the fact that Guerra did not have a computer password and wasn't authorized to receive a P.O. number. Nor would Guerra have easy access to mail going to another department located in a different part of the county. Quinn could not uncover any evidence to show that Guerra had an accomplice at Public Works or that he made a practice of hanging around the mail room in hopes of ferreting out P.O. numbers while remaining unobserved. Quinn knew that any of the foregoing scenarios were conceivable as chance events, but she could not find convincing proof through a preponderance of evidence that justified depriving Guerra of his job.

## THE DECISION

Quinn delivered her report to County Manager Dominic Dominguez, who read Quinn's recommendation that Guerra be given a letter of reprimand as the first step in progressive discipline. The county manager exploded in a rage: "No way—Guerra must be made an example of what happens to employees who steal!" Dominguez continued that it will be the county's position that Guerra obtained access to an existing P.O. number in order to bill the county for a portable toilet used at his personal residence. He intended to prove that Guerra thereby falsified information, defrauded the county, and subsequently was dishonest regarding his actions. Although the county does not put forth a specific theory regarding how Guerra perpetrated his actions, Dominguez believed that the preponderance of evidence would support just cause for discharging Guerra.

Quinn attempted to argue with the county manager: "We can't win in a grievance hearing; it is Orlando Guerra's position that he was unjustly and unfairly charged based on totally circumstantial evidence." Quinn played the devil's advocate: "Look, Orlando Guerra admits ordering a portable toilet for his private property but denies that he ever intended to bill the county and will contend that Rita Olmas mistakenly mixed up his order form with one filed by a county employee three days previously." Quinn reasoned that the county would be unable to show through a preponderance of evidence that Guerra possessed the knowledge, inclination, or skills to secure a P.O. number even if he had so desired. All the evidence against Guerra was circumstantial.

The county manager would not be deterred by Quinn's argument; Guerra would be discharged immediately following a perfunctory "Loudermill" disciplinary predetermination hearing. Quinn then left his office in quiet despair.

## DISCUSSION

1. Discuss whether the county should pursue some type of action against Guerra for wrongdoing.

2. Which arguments and facts support Quinn's case for a letter of reprimand?

3. Which arguments and facts support the county manager's decision to forgo progressive discipline in lieu of summary discharge?

# 26

## SUMMARY DISCHARGE OR PROGRESSIVE DISCIPLINE?

# Road Rage Among the Tar Heels

*News reports say that "road rage" is on the brink of being certified as an official mental disorder by the American Psychiatric Association. Until now, most of us have assumed that drivers who cut us off and give us the finger are just irate swine. But no, they appear to be suffering from a mental disorder, just like schizophrenics.*

Unfortunately, one of the terms that achieved common usage in the media during the 1990s was "road rage," which explained the often deadly phenomenon whereby drivers would turn violent at the slightest provocation and assault other drivers who provoked them by careless tactics. These assaults might stem from excessive speeding, tailgating, drivers cutting each other off, reckless lane changes, or driving on the shoulder at a high speed; at other times the imagined spark for violence might be completely unknown. In a more fortunate situation, the response might be an obscene gesture or obscenity; at worst, the result could be homicide or serious injury. Sometimes road rage erupts unexpectedly from someone who seems an unlikely aggressor.

Such was the case involving Robert Kline, 36, who had been a physical education teacher, athletic director, and baseball coach at Carrington Middle School in Durham, North Carolina, for 11 years. Kline also served as a driver's education instructor and was in that capacity as he and two female students arrived at the intersection of Dairy Road and Route 86 on an overcast September morning. Kline became angered when another car cut them off, and he ordered the student driver to chase the other car, driven by Jim Mitchell, 23, of Hillsborough. When both cars came to a stop in neighboring Chapel Hill, Kline exited the car, exchanged words with Mitchell, then hit him in the face; Mitchell, whose nose was bloodied, drove off and Kline told the student to give chase again. A Chapel Hill police officer pulled them over for speeding, and Kline was arrested for assault and released on $400 bond. Kline was suspended without pay shortly thereafter.

Kline's aggressive reaction sent shock waves throughout the school and community, as well as among Kline's friends who felt his reaction was a total aberration. "I've never known him to act this way," said James Harvey, a Little League coach in Durham and friend of Kline's for 12 years. "He's always had an open mind and a big heart." Even Kline's victim, Mitchell, did not want to see him resign over it: "It was never my wish that he lose his job over it; I'm an aspiring teacher myself." However, Sally Ferguson, vice president of the Carrington PTA, protested, "Instructors have a responsibility to teach safe-driving skills, and having students chase after another car would not be considered safe driving." Albert Nerenberg, a local psychologist, observed that Kline's actions probably would not affect the two teens he was teaching, "because they've seen the consequences of road rage up close and will be more careful."

## DISCUSSION

1.    You are the principal of Carrington Middle School and must decide how to handle the Robert Kline situation. Clearly you have the administrative discretion to discharge Kline from his duties as athletic director, baseball coach, and driver's education instructor or administer some form of less severe progressive discipline. However, Kline is tenured as a faculty member in physical education and your disciplinary options are less clear.

2.   You are the president of the local chapter of the Durham
     Teachers Association (DTA), and Robert Kline has
     approached you regarding his options should he be dis-
     charged. What advice do you give him? What do you say
     to your critics within the DTA who will be critical if you
     are not willing to defend "brother" Kline with all
     resources possible?

# 27

## MANAGING THE TRADITIONAL WORKER

# Billy Goat or Old Goat?

*There's this mentality in Recreation Services that is called the "wet T-shirt syndrome"—it's all fun and games as long as you're one of the young, fit crowd. But they don't feel the same way about us old farts; they make sexual innuendoes, and they snap bra and bathing suit strings all the time, but just let one of us old-timers try that and they cry "foul."*

Anselmo Bryan was hired by Salt Lake City, Utah, on or about July 1, 1972, and was continuously employed by the city directly or through federally funded grants administered by the city since his date of hire until his dismissal on the effective date of September 19, 1997. Bryan was placed on paid administrative leave on September 8, 1997, and subsequently attended a disciplinary predetermination hearing on September 15, 1997, that was conducted by Juan Vasquez; Ira Bolnicky represented Bryan at that hearing. The story of Bryan is one of an older worker, still caught in a time warp of the 1970s, who failed to adapt to the new realities of the workplace as the next millennium approached.

## BRYAN'S FIRING

The city fired Bryan on September 19 as a result of a series of alleged actions involving sexual harassment. Specifically, on July 24, 1997, Equal Employment Opportunity Commission (EEOC) Officer Renata Torreon received notice of a complaint that Bryan had inappropriately touched female employees at the Recreation Services Division (RSD). Torreon conducted an investigation of the allegations by interviewing a number of RSD employees. Following her investigation, Torreon wrote the following letter to Bryan:

> You were allowed an opportunity to respond to the various allegations during a meeting with me on July 31, 1997. As you are aware, certain female employees in the Recreation Services Division reported that you have, during the workday, patted them on the arm and rubbed their shoulders. In one instance, you rubbed a female employee's leg. Your conduct and actions were inappropriate, unprofessional, and could be construed to constitute sexual harassment in the workplace.

In addition, Torreon's review of pertinent records demonstrated that, while Bryan was working as the acting director at the Mosquito Abatement Division (MAD) in 1993, female employees reported nearly identical acts. Thus, the incidents for which Bryan was dismissed occurred in 1993 and 1997; the former incidents ultimately resulted in the administration of a letter of reprimand and the latter incidents culminated with Bryan's dismissal.

## 1993/1994 INCIDENTS

The first incident, which occurred in 1993, did not involve a victim who complained of sexually harassing behavior. Although it did not rise to the level of disciplinary action, Bryan and a female employee were observed by Malcolm Fletcher in a staff meeting on May 25, 1993, to be touching in an inappropriate manner. Specifically, Fletcher noted for the record that "in several instances Anselmo touched Helen Soto on the wrist or on the back to emphasize a point he had made." Fletcher counseled Bryan against this type of touching. Bryan seemed confused, "I don't understand. Helen and I have been friends since the first grade; we see nothing wrong in touching each other as friends."

In September/October of 1993, Bryan was assigned temporarily as acting director of MAD. During that period, two employees, Mercedes Reynolds and Deborah Pearson, filed complaints with the city's EEOC officer, Brenda Thomas, regarding Bryan's touching them on the back, arms, and shoulders, particularly when he stood close to these women while they were working. Thomas subsequently conducted an investigation, which included interviews with the two complainants, a MAD officer, the assistant division director, and Bryan. Thomas's finding was: "Part of Ms. Reynolds's allegations and most of Ms. Pearson's allegations have been substantiated by Mr. Bryan himself. He admits to touching women, but says that he doesn't consider his behavior to be sexual harassment because he had no sexual intent." Bryan stated that "he was from the old school" and didn't think touching while in conversation constituted sexual harassment.

Thomas and Fletcher met with Bryan on October 19. As a result of the complaints from MAD employees, Thomas conducted an investigation. Following Thomas's investigation, Bryan received a written reprimand and was provided training from Thomas regarding sexual harassment and touching in the workplace. Their assessment was that Bryan did not understand that his propensity to touch others was not always appreciated, especially by younger women; it could be construed as unwelcome sexual harassment. Thomas met with Bryan in her office to conduct a "refresher" course regarding elements of sexual harassment; this session involved review of a videotape and a discussion with Thomas. As a consequence of these actions, Bryan was given a letter of reprimand on December 3, 1993, because of his "inappropriate conduct and comments involving poor judgment during the period of September 20, 1993, and October 8, 1993."

Another incident occurred on May 26, 1994, with Hope Cordova, a city employee. Following an investigation by Thomas, it was concluded that Bryan made an insensitive comment "which does not constitute the hostile work environment form of sexual harassment." Bryan subsequently apologized and the matter was considered closed.

## 1997 INCIDENTS

On July 21, 1997, Stephanie Scott, 14 years of age at the time and a volunteer employee with the RSD, was asked to assist Bryan transfer files on his computer. While sitting next to Bryan, who was at his computer, Scott stated that Bryan would touch her back and shoulders. This would be followed by rubbing or patting them. Although these actions made her uncomfortable, Scott returned to work with Bryan on the following day; she indicated that Bryan again placed his hands on her shoulder, rubbed her back longer, and brushed his hand against her thigh. Scott indicated that Bryan's actions made her uncomfortable but that she did not say anything to him.

That evening, Scott told her mother, Juanita Albert—who also happened to be an employee in the RSD—about Bryan's actions. The following day, Albert informed her supervisor, Joann Catron, and Rudy Gomez, the department's assistant director, about the incidents. Catron and EEOC Officer Torreon, who asked Scott to put her statement in writing, subsequently interviewed Scott.

When interviewed by Torreon regarding the incidents with her daughter, Albert informed Torreon that Bryan was "a very touchy person" and had also touched her on the shoulder and moved too close when they were speaking together. (Albert stated that she had also witnessed Bryan put his hand on Scott's shoulders inappropriately.) However, Albert had never told Bryan, who was not her supervisor, that his actions were unwanted or made her feel uncomfortable.

Following the complaint by Scott, Catron, and later Torreon, interviewed Melinda Gomer, who formerly worked for the RSD, but did not report to Bryan. Melinda Gomer stated that Bryan would touch her on the arms and shoulders during conversations or while assisting with her work. Gomer indicated that his touching made her feel very uncomfortable but that she did not say anything to Bryan or wish to get him in trouble.

Valerie Herrera stated that Bryan had rubbed her shoulders in a manner that made her feel uncomfortable and had patted her arm and back. Herrera had worked for the RSD in the Before and After School/Summer Program, but she did not report Bryan's actions to her supervisor. Herrera did not complain to Bryan or anyone else concerning his behavior.

Corina Connor, an administrative assistant with the RSD, did not report to Bryan but worked with him on an occasional basis. Connor stated that Bryan would place his hands on her shoulders when engaged in conversation and that this made her uneasy. As a result, Connor decided to confront Bryan and asked him not to touch her; she stated that Bryan apologized and promised not to do so in the future (even though he slipped once and immediately apologized for doing so). Connor discussed the incident with Art Crum, the department director, and Catron at the time. Connor subsequently documented the incident on July 28, 1997, at the request of Catron. Connor did not file a complaint and considered the matter closed at the time.

Catron, who supervised Bryan and Albert, stated that she became involved in the investigation following Scott's complaint. Catron indicated that Bryan would stand a couple of feet away when they were engaged in conversation and that he never touched or patted her. Catron also testified that she had never found it necessary to counsel with Bryan because of his actions prior to these incidents. Catron was aware that Bryan used hearing aids and sometimes stood very close to hear soft-spoken individuals.

## BRYAN'S DEFENSE

Bryan was shocked at the allegations against him and believed that he was misunderstood because of several factors: (1) he was from a different generation than most of his coworkers, (2) he was misinterpreted because of his hearing impairment, and (3) his cultural background encouraged touching and hugging.

### Intergenerational Differences

Bryan's position was that he had never been the supervisor of those women who complained of sexual harassment.

Thus, he had no authority to make employment decisions that affected them nor did he ever make an inappropriate proposal for sexual favors to anyone. Furthermore, Bryan maintained that it was not clear that his touching created "an intimidating, hostile, or offensive work environment." When questioned, most women interviewed said that his touching made them feel "uncomfortable" but none complained of a hostile work environment that interfered with their job performance. In fact, only one individual, Connor, asked Bryan not to touch her, and he apologized and immediately complied with her request.

Bryan quipped that had he been young and handsome, "No one would have complained about my touching; instead, I was old, fat, and a Baptist in the capital city of the Mormons. I simply treated these women like I do the good Christian ladies at Mt. Olive Baptist Church, and they complained."

**Hearing Impairment**

Bryan also contended that his hearing impairment necessitated that he stand close in conversation or sit near the monitor when working with someone on the computer. Bryan requires the use of hearing aids in both ears. Occasionally, he asks for questions to be repeated and stands close in order to be understood. Touching is part of his nonverbal communication. When asked by Bryan's attorney, the following individuals affirmed Bryan's hearing problem:

1. *Liz Peralta*, a city administrative officer, indicated that Bryan had touched her on the shoulder or arms during conversations but never in a way that was personal or sexual in nature. She believed that Bryan did so because he was trying "to hang on to every word."

2. *Jamelle Morgan*, city public information officer, stated that Bryan stands close to people when speaking because of his hearing problem; he also pats men and women on the shoulder and touches them, but not in an inappropriate manner.

3. *Bernadette Jaworsky* indicated that Bryan would stand close to her because of his hearing problem and that he

touches both men and women during conversations but not inappropriately. Jaworsky also stated that touching among employees is quite common at RSD.

## Cultural Values

Bryan claimed that it is a part of his socialization as an African American male growing up in the South to touch and embrace individuals during conversation. The following individuals signed an affidavit confirming that Bryan is a "touchy person" and that they do not believe any sexual overtones are implied when he touches them:

1.  *John Henry*, who had worked with Bryan for 25 years, stated that Bryan would occasionally touch men and women in conversation, "as a black thing," but not as a sexual act.
2.  *Michael A. Garnet*, who had worked with Bryan for a number of years, stated that Bryan would touch him on the back, shoulder, or arm in a way that was typical of Southern African American males.
3.  *Wayne W. Zanos*, city budget and planning officer, stated that he had never observed Bryan touching in an unprofessional manner and that is was quite common in RSD for employees to hug, touch, and embrace one another.

## DISCUSSION

1.  Discuss Bryan's values and perspectives as a coworker. In what ways are they contributing to generational conflicts at work?
2.  Decide whether Bryan's problems stem primarily from a generational or a gender perspective.
3.  Assume Salt Lake City reconsidered its decision and reinstated Bryan to a new position in another department. You are Bryan's supervisor and much younger in age. What advice would you give to him?

# 28

## CONFLICT RESOLUTION AND
## GRIEVANCE HANDLING

# Too Many Christmas Carols in the Winter Festival

*We invite you to consider membership in the new employee association known as ACROSS, Association of Christians Reaching Out in Service and Support, which was recently recognized as an official employee organization. According to the approved charter (see below), any employee, retiree, individual, or family member who supports the Association's purposes and goals may join. Among our purposes are:*

- *To contribute to employee welfare and morale by supporting and strengthening one another in the practice of a living faith in Jesus Christ, devoted to serving our fellow employees and agency constituents.*

- *To unite Christians and those who support the principles of the Christian religion, within the local workplace as well as those widely separated geographically.*

Fred Rotelli, music teacher and choir director at Highland High School, faced what he believed to be a test of his faith in Jesus Christ with the secular "new age" dictates of the school district administrators. It was Rotelli's responsibility to lead the high school choir in the annual "winter concert," which coincidentally happened to fall six days before Christmas Day. Rotelli had originally planned to conduct a "Christmas Concert" in December 1997 that would include a solo performance of "O Holy Night," but was persuaded by district administrators to pull it at the last minute. Rotelli was determined, as a matter of his Christian witness, to keep as much Christian Christmas as possible, even though he had also compromised by agreeing to change the name of the concert to a Winter Festival. Elizabeth Lincoln, Highland's principal, suggested to Rotelli that he might consider more secular themes focusing on Santa Claus, Rudolph, Silver Bells, and Frosty, rather than songs that directly spoke to the birth of Jesus Christ. Rotelli was not amused by the request and had no intention to downplay the biblical account of Christmas. So, despite Principal Lincoln's not so subtle "request" to make further deletions of Christmas carols from the proposed performance, Rotelli could not in good conscience make additional concessions that he considered would be secularizing Christmas. Two weeks prior to the concert, several Highland parents signed a petition objecting to Rotelli's performance and calling for his immediate dismissal if he continued to refuse to make changes in the Winter Festival program.

On Friday, December 19, the student choir held its Winter Festival performance, during which students sang more than 15 numbers, approximately half of which contained Christian themes. Even though Rotelli suggested to the choir that they omit the name "Jesus" in the opening song, the Christian students in the choir decided to go ahead and repeat the phrase "Jesus, there is no Christmas without you" more than a dozen times. Following the 90-minute concert, several parents were quite upset with Rotelli's actions. They were distraught that the concert failed to include any songs that referred to Hanukkah, Kwanza, Ramadan, or any other religious holiday.

This was not the first time that Rotelli had defied district administrative orders that he believed to be contradictory to his own Christian beliefs. The district had passed a policy in May regarding the separation of religion from regular school activity. In unequivocal terms, the district had mandated that, "schools should be religion neutral, neither promoting nor inhibiting religious beliefs, so as to assure comfort to all students." Soon thereafter, the district announced the following changes to the social studies curriculum:

- The abbreviation "A.D." preceding a year, e.g., A.D. 32, would no longer be interpreted as 32 years following the death of Christ (*anno Domini*, "in the year of the Lord"); henceforth, "A.D." would be changed to "C.E." ("of the common era").

- The abbreviation "B.C." following a year, e.g., 100 B.C., would no longer be read as "before Christ"; henceforth, B.C. would be changed to "B.C.E." ("before the common era").

Rotelli, a senior social studies instructor, had announced to his classes that he would not be complying with the district's directive to replace A.D. and B.C. with C.E. and B.C.E.; he also considered it an abridgement of his rights as a citizen under the First Amendment to the Constitution, which states, "Congress shall make no law respecting an establishment of religion, or prohibiting the free exercise thereof; . . ." The school board, in a split decision of 4 to 3, ordered the district superintendent to issue a letter of reprimand to Rotelli for insubordination.

Nor did Rotelli's problems end with his defiance of district policy on religious neutrality. On other occasions, Rotelli would explain to his classes the meanings of various religious holidays such as Easter, Passover, Lent, and Good Friday. Rotelli would also pause for a moment of silence at the beginning of each class to express thanks for his blessings and world peace. For these actions, Rotelli received several verbal warnings and letters of instruction.

Following the Christmas program incident, the superintendent decided that the school had been subjected to enough of what was considered to be Rotelli's arrogance and insubordination under the guise of religious expression. On January 29, the superintendent decided to fire Rotelli and, in a termination letter, stated that this decision was based "on his usual difficulties with administration policies." Rotelli's impending dismissal provoked a firestorm of protest that received national coverage in the media, including the *Rush Limbaugh Show* and *The 700 Club*. Attorneys from the

American Center for Law and Justice, a firm founded by tel-
evangelist Pat Robertson, contacted Rotelli and pledged to
take his religious infringement case to federal court. The
chair of the school board received massive numbers of post-
cards, phone calls, letters, and E-mail from all over the
United States and Canada.

A few days later, the school board met in closed session
for five hours with Rotelli, his attorneys, the superintendent,
and the district's attorney in an effort to reach a settlement.
Even though the board could have upheld the superintendent's decision to discharge Rotelli, it was concerned about
the potential for negative publicity and potential litigation
costs. Finally, an agreement was reached by which Rotelli
agreed to resign voluntarily and not sue the district on the
grounds that it infringed on his religious liberties. In return,
the school board agreed to clear Rotelli's personnel record of
all disciplinary action. Rotelli was quoted as saying that he
was pleased because his name had been cleared and he had
been able to witness for his religious beliefs. The school board
chair announced that he was gratified that all parties were
able to reach a good solution to a very difficult and sensitive
problem.

## DISCUSSION

1.  Do you believe that the solution reached in this matter
    was fair to all parties or should the school district have
    used the opportunity to stand firm on its policy regard-
    ing religious neutrality?

2.  How could this dispute possibly have been avoided?
    What roles might have been helpful in dispute resolu-
    tion for (1) the principal, (2) Fred Rotelli, and (3) the
    superintendent?

3.  How might mediation be used in this situation? Who
    could perform the mediator's role?

# 29

## ATTENDANCE MANAGEMENT

# What's a Single Mom to Do?

*Being a single mother has got to be the most difficult and thankless job in America. After all, many people still believe that it must be your fault that you couldn't keep your man. Then there are those judges who think that if you put your kid in a day care center in order to go back to school or work several jobs, you must be selfish and uncaring to do that to your child. Of course, you're also seen as selfish if you leave your child with a sitter while you go out on a date, assuming you can find a man who would want to date a woman with children. To top it all off, you've got some unsympathetic boss at work who can't understand why you should take sick leave when your child is sick and the day care center won't accept sick kids.*

## BACKGROUND

Janet Allen had never really thought that she would settle down in a place like Kingman, Arizona, located in the high desert; for most observers passing by, it was just a place to stop and eat or sleep on Interstate 40 (or old Route 66) as they journeyed across the continent. But Janet had married Tom Allen, a mechanic from Kingman, who had brought his new bride home in 1988. Within the year, Janet gave birth to daughter

Amanda, forcing her to quit work as an accounting technician with Bullhead City. Janet really wouldn't mind missing the commute to Bullhead City and was looking forward to staying home with her baby. Unfortunately, Janet's plans began to unravel quickly when Tom unexpectedly announced one morning that he was off to Nashville to make a career as a country singer and that he had decided that marriage and parenting would be too limiting for him in his newly chosen career.

After Tom left, Janet took action to rearrange her life so that she could work closer to home and spend more time with her daughter. She applied at several businesses and government agencies until finally she was hired as a records clerk with the Mojave County Sheriff's Department on July 24, 1989. For the next two years, Janet performed well in her job and she accumulated a substantial amount of sick leave to use in case she or her daughter should ever become ill. Janet's job as a records clerk was fairly mundane, and her supervisor allowed Janet to work on a flextime schedule so that Amanda could be taken to and picked up from a sitter at appropriate times.

On November 13, 1991, Janet applied for and was hired for a job-sharing position as a budget clerk with the county, a position that she shared with another single parent. Both individuals were able to work 20 hours per week and receive full benefits. This position proved to be ideal for Janet, and the extra time allowed her to complete an associate of arts degree as an accounting technician at Mojave Community College. Thus, armed with an A.A. degree and faced with a growing number of bills and no child support payments from her out-of-work ex-husband, Janet accepted a higher paying job as an accounting technician with Mojave County on February 20, 1995, in the county's Budget and Finance Department. However, the new job was much more structured and required Janet to be in her office for a full eight hours each day. To complicate matters, Amanda developed an asthmatic condition that caused her to stay home from school frequently. For each of these attacks, Janet used sick leave, and by 1996 had depleted her accrued sick leave. Occasionally, she was forced to request leave without pay to take care of Amanda because her sick leave and annual leave were completely exhausted, and her boss would not approve paid leave of any type.

Faced with a rising use of sick leave among county

employees at about the same time, County Administrator Gene Romolo promulgated Administrative Instruction No. 100, "Sick Leave Management Policy," on February 9, 1997. Pursuant to that policy, county employees were allowed to use up to 44 percent of their accrued sick leave amount for one year "without prejudice." After use of 44 percent, employees could be required to submit physicians' excuses if sickness occurred in conjunction with other scheduled days off. Sick leave would be accrued at a rate of eight hours per month. Each county department head was delegated authority by the county administrator to set policies and procedures for employees to follow when requesting sick leave approval. Each department head could approve or disapprove requests for sick leave. The Accounting Division Handbook required an employee to contact his or her supervisor no later than one-half hour prior to the start of intended sick leave usage. If the supervisor should be unavailable, the employee was instructed to leave a message for the supervisor to return the call.

Janet's attendance had continued to deteriorate throughout 1996 and early 1997 as her daughter's condition worsened, and Janet used all of her available sick leave. When Janet's supervisor, Tim Briggs, warned Janet that sick leave was intended for employee sickness, not for their children, Janet simply stated that she had no other choice and had to take care of her child. In March 1997, Janet received her first letter of warning for sick leave overutilization; by April, Janet had been given two letters of reprimand for the same reason. Faced with what seemed to be an impossible dilemma between work requirements and child-rearing demands, Janet requested a voluntary transfer placement to a position in another unit, which hopefully had a more sympathetic supervisor. Fortunately, a similar position opened up in the Purchasing Division of the same department.

In May 1997, Janet transferred from the Budget Office to the Purchasing Division. On May 15, Janet's new supervisors Marshall Morgan and Yvonne Smith discussed her previous sick leave usage in the Budget Office, and although they were willing to grant Janet a tabula rasa regarding her past attendance record, both emphasized that Janet's sick leave usage in the Purchasing Division would need to decrease and her pattern of using a majority of her sick leave days in conjunction with scheduled days off should cease.

Alas, the same situation persisted for Janet as the following series of incidents occurred throughout 1997:

*June 2:* Janet received a verbal warning regarding excessive sick leave usage. She was informed that she could expect to receive progressive discipline in the future if her sick leave usage remained high. Janet was also counseled by her supervisors regarding possible solutions for the causes of her sick leave usage.

*June 23:* Janet was cautioned by her supervisors regarding excessive sick leave use and unscheduled vacation use. Janet was aware that she might be absent on June 24, because of medical complications, but she did not take this opportunity to tell her supervisors of this possibility.

*June 24, 25, and 26:* Janet did not call her supervisors in order to request sick leave.

*June 25:* Janet was sent a written warning regarding her sick leave usage and failure to follow proper procedures when calling in.

*July 1:* Janet attended a predisciplinary hearing concerning her excessive absenteeism. Janet subsequently received a five-day suspension without pay, which was to be served at a mutually agreeable time over the next five months. This suspension was later appealed to a grievance hearing.

*July 7:* Janet was reminded to contact her supervisors before the start of work when seeking sick leave.

*July 10:* Janet was cautioned about excessive sick leave use on her performance evaluation in July 1997.

*October 13:* The personnel hearing officer convened a grievance hearing to consider the five-day suspension of Janet for excessive sick leave abuse. After convening the hearing, both parties agreed to a reduced disciplinary settlement of two-and-one-half days. Janet was also warned that continued sick leave abuse would result in a more serious discipline. The county administrator approved this settlement on October 27, 1997.

Despite the settlement arrangement, Amanda continued to experience frequent asthma attacks and Janet's overutilization of sick leave was unabated. During October and November, the following sequence of events occurred:

*October 24:* Janet was absent from work because of sickness and did not call her supervisors within 30 minutes following the start of work.

*October 31 and November 3:* Janet took two days sick leave but did not properly notify her supervisors. Janet took scheduled vacation leave on November 4, 1997.

## THE DECISION TO DISCIPLINE A SINGLE MOM

A review of her personnel records revealed that Janet used 213 percent of her accrued sick leave from February 1997 through November 1997. July was the only month during this period when Janet did not use sick leave. In August, September, October, and November 1997, Janet used more than her accrued sick leave for each of those months. An initial predetermination hearing was scheduled for November 10, by written memorandum, dated November 4, 1997; Janet was informed that her sick leave usage and work history would be topics for discussion at the predetermination hearing.

At her predetermination or so-called "Loudermill" hearing, Janet was given an opportunity to present any new facts or circumstances to explain her overutilization of sick leave and to offer reasons why the county should not discipline her. Janet did not exercise her "Weingarten" right, which permits a bargaining unit member to have a union representative at a disciplinary hearing. At the beginning of the meeting, the county administrator explained that sick leave is unscheduled leave intended solely for a very specific purpose—sickness. When sick leave patterns by a particular employee emerge, management has a right—even an obligation—to monitor usage. Mojave County has both the right to ensure that sick leave is being properly used and an obligation to monitor patterns that suggest possible misuse. The administrator stated that the fact that approximately 80 percent of Janet's sick leave had occurred in conjunction with days off—weekends, holidays, annual leave, school holidays, and the like—suggested sick leave "abuse" rather than simple "overutilization" by Janet.

At the conclusion of the hearing, Janet surprised everyone present by stating that she intended to take off November 12, 1997, regardless of the hearing's outcome, to spend time with her daughter. Marshall Morgan took the opportunity to inform Janet that the county was considering terminating her because of four considerations:

1. Her continued overutilization of sick leave following her transfer

2. Her abuse of sick leave by overlapping weekends and vacation days

3. Her lack of response to previous corrective efforts

4. Morgan's perception, based in part on her request for additional leave during the predetermination hearing, that Janet was not motivated to change her pattern of sick leave use

After listening to Morgan, Janet shrugged her shoulders and stated that her daughter was frequently sick and child care undependable. Janet said, "I think the county needs to be more family friendly; I'm a single mom who must bear the entire burden of raising a child with special medical needs; I would hope the county could be more understanding and let me work a flex schedule." Morgan replied that other employees in the Purchasing Division whose sick leave usage exceeded 44 percent of accrued sick leave were either counseled or disciplined. Morgan asserted that Janet's productivity and the division's productivity suffered because of her absenteeism. The time period beginning in July is the busiest part of the year for the division, and everyone is needed at work.

The county subsequently terminated Janet on November 11, following her predetermination hearing. The letter of termination from the county stated that, in determining an appropriate action to take with Janet, the county considered progressive discipline. However, Janet claimed that termination was noncorrective of her sick leave problem and too severe as a disciplinary action. Janet later decided to grieve the county's disciplinary decision on four grounds:

1.  That her performance was satisfactory, except for sick leave overutilization

2.  That Chief Administrative Officer Gene Romolo exceeded his policy-making authority in February 1997, when he effectively took away sick leave rights for all county employees

3.  That, compared to other employees, she suffered disparate treatment by her supervisors, who denied her request to take accrued sick leave and that she was not counseled to go to the County Wellness Center

4.  That she was denied due process rights because of an improperly conducted predetermination hearing, in which she was not informed of her right to have a union representative present

## DISCUSSION

1.  Does Janet's absenteeism present any mitigating circumstances that should be considered by management, or should she be treated the same as all other employees regarding attendance policies?

2.  In your assessment, does Janet's use of sick leave represent "overutilization" or "abuse" of sick leave? What is the significance of both and what difference does it make?

3.  Has management acted in a punitive manner with Janet? What other options, if any, might be offered by management?

# 30

## COMPARATIVE HRM

# Human Resources Management in the Land of the Czars

*In 1997, Tara Sather went on a Rotary International Exchange Fellowship to study public administration in Kirov, Russia. The following composite excerpts from her E-mail correspondence provide insights into the theory and practice of human resources management in the former land of the Czars.*

## SATURDAY, 8 NOVEMBER 1997

WOW! Three months, four systems, and two phones later, I think I now have a pretty reliable E-mail system here in my apartment. I could write a book on public administration here just relating the song and dance of trying to get this hooked up.

The ubiquitous response of Russians to the statement that I'm a public administration [PA] student studying here is genuine, strong laughter. I must say honestly I'm learning more from just being here, listening and asking questions, than I'm learning in classes. I'm in a management class taught by someone whose last management over anything was in a Soviet ministry, a marketing class being taught by

195

someone who has never written a marketing plan, a law class that everyone I've talked to agrees is pretty useless since laws here don't mean much anymore, and a class on world culture that is quite interesting but has no relation to PA.

I am one of the first international students they've had here as well as one of the only grad students in this university. It is a new university—only been around three years. It's on the grounds of an old Soviet military academy, and a lot of the administration comes to Kirov only once or twice a week from Moscow. Their Kirov work is only one of several jobs they now have. The plan for most grad students in Kirov is to have their own projects on which they work with professors in the field. So what I've done is to attempt to establish two projects with professors at the university. They have taken a while to get rolling, but I'm sure learning along the way.

It's just so overwhelming to see the differences in how things work here and in the States—large and small. A "small thing" example: In classified ads here, where companies are advertising for positions, it is very common to have specific sex and age requirements listed in the first line of the job requirements:

- Man, 30–40 years old, wanted for position of international lawyer in trading company
- Woman, 27–40 years old, wanted for position of secretary of economic credit in such and so bank

A "large thing" example: It appears that most Russian companies' idea of a personnel management program is to instill fear in the workers, so people are afraid to do anything on their own initiative, take risks, or question anything. Managers should be both far above the workers and uncommunicative to encourage this fear and obedience in those working for them. Record keeping on personnel is not deemed necessary.

I'm trying to be careful about giving suggestions. I vacillate between saying, "Geez, folks, if you want to get into the international business and government community, you gotta change some of this," and remembering that I am a foreigner here; Russia's been around a lot longer than the

United States, and who am I really to suggest how they run things? It's encouraging to see differences in international companies working in Moscow, but how fast that influence will spread is hard to tell; setting up a good personnel administration program takes time and is not easy. If managers are neither used to having nor required to have such a program, then there seems to be little reason to establish one. Even trying to explain the reasons for having a PA program are hard to sell to people who are not accustomed to managing this way. It seems to be a fear of a loss of control and power, and a strong line between workers and managers is so ingrained here it's going to require at least one generation to really change things, I believe.

One of the professors in the university is involved in social work in Russia. Just last week I went south of Moscow to see a social services center that is one of three such centers in Russia. It was originally established by UNESCO, but it has since needed to find its own funding. Now the city budget is funding a basic pay for the psychologists working there, but there were eight months that they worked without pay. The center has about 32 group meetings a week, in addition to private consultations. The groups are everything from pensioners to disabled children, to teaching teenagers about sex, to parent and child family counseling groups and training local teachers. There is a need for even more work—for example, to have groups on drug addiction, programs for children . . . the issues are just more than one center can begin to deal with.

It's amazing what this one center is doing in this community. Even more amazing, though, is that this is one of THREE in Russia. I asked, "what happens in the cities that don't have such a center?" The workers just kind of got a blank look on their faces and said—"Nothing." They are also struggling with the differences in administration between private and public organizations, struggling in administration between the main manager who is older and afraid to try anything new and a young group of people under her who want to try things but can't get anywhere because she refuses to try. I took pages of notes and could go on for days, but the whole idea of attempting to set up a program for social work in such a huge country where nothing has been before, where there is no structure for social programs, no established funding for such things, and problems emerging that have never had dealt with before. . . . It is just overwhelming. I'm curious now to talk to some of the people in Kirov and see what type of programs are here. I know there are some, but from what I've seen, most of what is done is at least initiated by foreign programs and funds. This country can't be dependent on that money forever. A lot of the programs that are begun fall apart after the grant runs out, and the community is left with little more than they had previously.

## WEDNESDAY, 17 DECEMBER 1997

WOW has it been cold! Monday broke a 90+ year record low. I've been doing most of my studying in the bathtub room of my apartment because, thanks to the hot-water pipes, it's by far the warmest room here. I've heard December and January are the coldest months of the year, so I'm taking a deep breath and will try and plow through!

I have compiled quite a bit of information on changing management practices here. Now I need to get the information all juggled around and put in a sensical order. There are so many different opinions, differing reactions, and divergent visions of the future! It's hugely interesting, but just overwhelming at times.

## WEDNESDAY, 28 JANUARY 1998

More greetings from Russia. Just a few hours ago, I returned from a meeting with the Policies and Practices Subcommittee of the Human Resources Committee of the American Chamber of Commerce (AMCham) in Moscow. AMCham has been here since 1991, when they were set up to support a forum for networking and sharing experiences among American organizations in Moscow. AMCham has set a number of committees, the largest of which is the Human Resources Committee, with about 50 members. One of their subcommittees is the Policies and Practices Subcommittee, which has identified six HR issues of concern:

- *Social Fund Issues:* What do companies *know* about it and how have they worked with it?

- *Travel Expenses:* This is an especially touchy issue in Russia because of crazy tax laws affecting travel compensation.

- *Benefits:* Of particular concern is how organizations can provide lunches/lunch time and use of company cars. Secondly, the health care system in Russia is hampered by overlapping and inefficient payment plans. It also faces serious misinformation or noninformation among the general population on basic health issues as well as various health problems that change from region to region.

- *Discipline:* What can organizations do about employee theft and abuse of sick time? Also, what is the legal status of employee termination? If employees take a termination to court, what sort of documentation is needed or expected?

- *Moscow Registration:* There is a Moscow law that states that foreign organizations working in Moscow are not allowed to hire anyone not officially living in Moscow. This law was passed to "protect" Moscow from the influx of non-residents coming to the capital hoping to find better-paying jobs. While already challenged and declared unconstitutional in Russian court, the law is still being enforced by overzealous militia and labor inspectors. Several foreigners have already been "made aware" of this law, and the committee chair remarked during the meeting, "Wow, I didn't know about this law; it looks like I'll have to fire about half of my employees."

- *Hiring and Recruitment of New Employees:* There are numerous restrictions regarding the hiring of students and expatriates, especially if they are believed to be hired over Russians who can do the same jobs. There is a serious unemployment problem, which is particularly interesting because this issue did not officially exist in Soviet times. Now the unemployment problem ties in with homelessness, unpaid wages, and the need to retrain workers.

As you can see, true human resources management has a long way to go in the former land of Czars, but it is fascinating to be in on the ground floor as it is being built.

## DISCUSSION

1.  What advice would you offer to Sather regarding how assertive she might become in offering her opinions on modern practices in HRM?

2.  In your opinion, should AMCham's Human Resources Committee continue with its present study agenda or assume a more neutral posture concerning HRM issues?

3.  Which of the HR problems facing American organizations in Russia should be addressed by short-term and which by long-term strategies?

CASES IN PUBLIC HUMAN RESOURCE MANAGEMENT
Edited by John Beasley
Production supervision by Kim Vander Steen
Cover design by Jeanne Calabrese Design, River Forest, Illinois
Composition by Precision Typographers, Michigan City, Indiana
Paper, Finch Opaque
Printed and bound by McNaughton & Gunn, Saline, Michigan